Healthcare Transformation

The purpose of this book is to offer health system board members an actionable, concise guide on their role, as well as, provide updates on key changes in healthcare delivery, including evidence and contemporary examples.

The goal is for any board member to have an opportunity to not only be literate in healthcare but also to be supportive and engaged in the transformation of their organization and the industry toward improving health. Hospital and health system board members, regardless of their experience and expertise, are challenged with keeping pace with healthcare performance and strategy. Surveys continue to show that this is not their comfort level, given healthcare complexity and the rate of recent change and targets for transformation. The aim of this book is to keep the guide concise so that all board members can become fairly literate on the major issues, with an emphasis on recent updates in healthcare, for today and the future.

This is an ideal book for new board members for their orientation to the board and for all board members to use to have a knowledge base and a set of questions to facilitate their engagement on these important issues. Much has changed since the initial printing of *Healthcare Transformation* in 2009, and this second edition provides updated resources and more contemporary examples and lessons for both new and seasoned board members. This edition updates all chapters and provides three new transformers/chapters to consider.

Maulik Joshi is the President and CEO of Meritus Health. Meritus Health includes the proposed Meritus School of Osteopathic Medicine and Meritus Medical Center. He has a Doctorate in public health from the University of Michigan. He has authored a combination of over 50 peer-reviewed articles, commentaries, books, and perspectives. Maulik serves on numerous boards within and outside of healthcare.

Aaron George is Associate Dean for Clinical Education for the proposed Meritus School of Osteopathic Medicine. He holds a medical degree from the Philadelphia College of Osteopathic Medicine in Philadelphia, and his residency in family medicine from Duke University Medical Center in Durham, North Carolina. Dr. George is an author and has been a speaker on population health, medical education, and physician leadership development throughout the spectrum of clinical training.

Healthcare Transformation
A Guide for the Health System Board Member
Second Edition

Maulik Joshi, Dr.P.H.
Aaron George, D.O.

Foreword by Richard J. Pollack,
President and CEO,
American Hospital Association

Routledge
Taylor & Francis Group

A PRODUCTIVITY PRESS BOOK

First published 2025
by Routledge
605 Third Avenue, New York, NY 10158

and by Routledge
4 Park Square, Milton Park, Abingdon, Oxon, OX14 4RN

Routledge is an imprint of the Taylor & Francis Group, an informa business

First edition published by Routledge 2009

ISBN: 978-1-032-79796-0 (hbk)
ISBN: 978-1-032-79795-3 (pbk)
ISBN: 978-1-003-49391-4 (ebk)

DOI: 10.4324/9781003493914

Typeset in Garamond
by SPi Technologies India Pvt Ltd (Straive)

Contents

Foreword

Behind every great healthcare organization is a great board. "Beside" may be a better description of their place, since today's most effective boards are working more closely than ever with healthcare leaders at every level as trusted partners to ensure that their organization meets its mission – delivering compassionate and healing care that is safe, timely, effective, efficient, and equitable for all patients.

For members of hospital or health system boards, the privilege of serving as a steward to carry out the healthcare organization's mission is more important than ever as healthcare continues to rapidly transform. This ranges from regulatory demands and emerging technological evolutions to challenging financing models.

While duties such as fiduciary responsibilities remain foundational for boards, trustees also should understand the complexities of healthcare, including trends, regulations, and best practices that can improve patient care. This can be challenging for seasoned board members and may be confusing for new members.

With *Healthcare Transformation: A Guide for the Health System Board Member*, Maulik Joshi and Aaron George have met this need for an informative and practical guide to support board members in their role of helping their organizations navigate the restless waters of healthcare transformation, and ensure that their organizations have the resources needed to continue providing quality care to their patients and communities.

This second edition concisely presents the ten major transformers already driving healthcare in the first decades of the twenty-first century and shows how Boards can understand and use them to transform their own organizations.

It also assists in developing the necessary trustee competencies for organizational success. Each chapter presents practical information which helps demystify the current healthcare environment and provides direction to boards as they steer their organization's course through the ever-changing challenges and obstacles in healthcare.

This updated edition also examines the crucial role of boardroom culture in leveraging their board members' perspectives and experience, resulting in a stronger board and a stronger organization.

Whether you refer to this guide as a board member, executive, or student of healthcare governance, consider how this approach to transformation can reinforce the strong bond of trust with our patients and communities.

Strengthening the knowledge and thought leadership of boards directly helps caregivers achieve their mission of advancing health for our patients and communities. This book is your guide.

Richard J. Pollack
President and CEO
American Hospital Association

Chapter 1

Introduction

Current Challenges in Healthcare

The quality, cost, and delivery of healthcare are increasingly paramount issues in the United States. These not only impact the lives of Americans but also the well-being of communities and the financial health of our state and federal governments. Over two decades ago, a wake-up call for health system change was provided by the Institute of Medicine (IOM) in its landmark report, *To Err Is Human: Building a Safer Health System* (IOM 2000). The report estimated that at the time between 44,000 and 98,000 people were dying each year because of medical error. Though the landscape has certainly changed, even into the 2020s, studies have suggested that as many as 1 in 10 patients may be harmed while receiving hospital care and at least 50% of the harm caused by adverse events is preventable (Leatherman & Berwick 2020). Meanwhile, the cost of delivering this care continues to skyrocket toward unsustainable levels. Where calls for constraining healthcare costs have been loud and clear since the 1960s, little has been effective at slowing the trajectory. As of 2022, healthcare costs consumed 17.3% of the entire US Gross Domestic Product (GDP). Perhaps most alarming, this equates to an annual spend of $13,493 for every man, woman, and child in America. Despite this, quality and delivery have not substantively improved (CMS 2023a).

Major challenges in healthcare quality are affecting patients, families, and providers and resulting in poor clinical outcomes. When compared to the 38 nations of the Organisation for Economic Co-Operation and Development

(OECD) the United States not only ranks last in preventable mortality, but its citizens have a 3-year lower life expectancy than the average (Gunja et al. 2023). Across 71 performance measures, the US ranks last overall, despite spending far more money relatively than the other 10 first-world nations including Germany, France, Canada, the United Kingdom, and others. In particular, the US ranked worst in access to care, administrative efficiency, equity, and healthcare outcomes (Schneider et al. 2021).

Variations in care are impacted by geography as well as social, cultural, and demographic circumstances. If you are a patient covered by Medicare living in Chicago, Illinois, you could expect an average annual beneficiary spend of $12,915. However, getting in a car and driving a little more than 2 hours south to Bloomington, Illinois you would find Medicare patients with figures of $8,631 (Cooper et al. 2022). Studies even show that a person's zip code affects their life expectancy more than their genetic code. And it is not even a close figure – the gap based on geography means that living in one location versus another leads to average life expectancies that span from 63 years to 96 years (Lowery 2022). Much of this has to do with the growing recognition that health is much more than a list of a patient's symptoms or illnesses. That is, health is impacted tremendously by social, family, community, workplace, financial, educational, and many other elements that have come to be collectively referred to as the social determinants of health.

Minorities, low-income, or uninsured adults and children are more likely to wait to seek care when sick; encounter delays and poorly coordinated care; and have untreated chronic diseases, avoidable hospitalizations, and worse outcomes. Technology and system coordination and communication could address many efficiency and quality concerns. These numbers and trends continue to change but are often in the wrong direction for the United States.

Challenges in healthcare were magnified through the COVID-19 pandemic experienced in the early part of the 2020s. Systems were pressed to their limits and forced to adapt to high patient volumes, unexpected and rapid changes, and substantial issues with staffing and team member burnout. Likewise, there were shifts in public trust, which had traditionally been quite high for the healthcare industry, and in particular with US federal, state, and local public health agencies as well as overall scientific credibility (SteelFisher et al. 2023).

Some advances are taking place with changes to traditional payment, policy, and infrastructure. These include efforts from payors like Medicare to try to financially incentivize organizations and providers to demonstrate better quality and outcomes. Also, advances have been seen in the science of quality improvement, particularly concerning best practices to address patient safety issues as will be identified in this book. Meanwhile, new and non-traditional entities are entering the healthcare delivery space, seeking to innovate as well as disrupt. Board and executive leadership are needed to guide change to improve systems of care at each hospital and healthcare organization. This need can be also seen in the following data:

- 26 days: The average time a patient waited in 2022 to get an appointment with a physician. This has gone in the wrong direction, up from 21 days in 2004, and 24.1 days in 2017 (Payerchin 2022).
- 8 hours: The time per month the average US adult spends coordinating healthcare for themselves and/or their family. This same survey showed that 65% of all adults feel managing healthcare is "overwhelming" and "time-consuming" (AAPA 2022).
- 25%: The segment of the US adult population who say they skipped or postponed getting healthcare that they needed because of the cost. That number jumps to an astonishing 61% for those who are uninsured (Kaiser 2023).
- 15%: The rate at which Medicare patients who are discharged from the hospital will return for readmission within 30 days (CMS 2023b). Concerningly, 1 in every 4 of those readmissions is preventable (Auerbach, Kripalani, & Vasilevskis 2016).
- 2 out of 3: The ratio of patients (67%) who would definitely recommend the hospital in which they received care (CMS 2023c).
- $760 billion: The estimated total minimum costs of waste in the US healthcare system, which could be as high as $935 billion. These come from failures in care delivery and care coordination, overtreatment, low-value care, fraud and abuse, and administrative complexity (Shrank, Rogstad, & Parekh 2019).

Your Duty

As a board member, you have a fiduciary role in the performance of your healthcare organization. This comes with accountability and obligation in how you carry out your governance role. Most important is to ensure that the mission of the organization is achieved. In some form, each organization has a mission that addresses community health improvement, quality and safety of patient care, customer/patient satisfaction, community benefit, and financial sustainability. Additionally, boards must continually respond to new clinical, operational, and regulatory developments associated with quality of care. This requires strategic thinking and anticipation of market disruption.

Board obligations concerning quality of care arise in two different areas:

1. The decision-making function: The application of the duty of care to a specific decision or particular board action (e.g., granting, restricting, or revoking privileges of members of the medical staff).
2. The oversight function: The application of the duty of care concerning overseeing operations (e.g., assuring that a reasonable quality information and medical error-reporting system exists) (Callender et al. 2007).

The problems identified earlier are related to the oversight function—the obligation you have as a board member to "keep a finger on the pulse" of the activities of the organization in addressing these and other quality issues. Concerning the oversight function, a joint publication from the U.S. Department of Health and Human Services and the American Health Lawyers Association (AHLA) states:

> The basic governance obligation to guide and support executive leadership in the maintenance of quality of care and patient safety is an ongoing task. Board members are increasingly expected to assess organizational performance on emerging quality of care concepts and arrangements as they implicate issues of patient safety, appropriate levels of care, cost reduction, reimbursement, and collaboration among providers and practitioners. These are all components of the oversight function
>
> (Callender et al. 2007)

Board members do not necessarily need to know everything about healthcare, but they must be equipped to ask the right questions at the right time and to act upon the answers. This book provides the background to understand those pressing issues and the framing to ask just those questions.

Need for Transformational Change and Leadership

Improving the health of the community they serve is the most basic and fundamental mission of almost every healthcare organization. To fulfill that mission and to address the issues identified earlier, we need to transform healthcare. Hence, this guide is about what you need to do to support the transformation of your organization to ensure quality, patient safety, sustainability, and advancement.

Incremental improvement is not enough to deal with long-standing quality issues. Incrementalism is too slow and will not address deep systems issues in healthcare. What is needed is transformational leadership that: (1) alters the culture of the institution by changing select underlying assumptions and institutional behaviors, processes, and products; (2) is deep and pervasive, affecting the whole institution; (3) is intentional; and (4) occurs over time (Eckel, Hill, and Green 1998).

The Top Ten Healthcare Transformers

The model in Figure 1.1 is the guide to transformation in your organization. As you see, there are ten healthcare transformers. A book chapter is devoted to each transformer and key aspects are highlighted below:

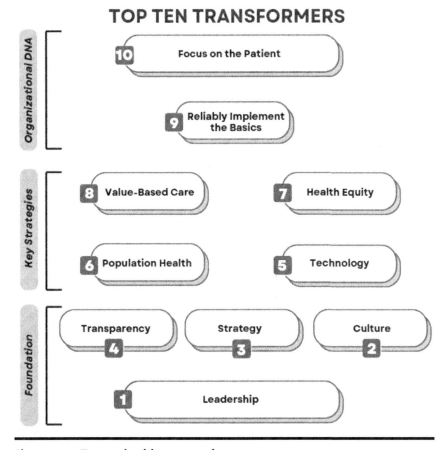

Figure 1.1   Top ten healthcare transformers.

Transformer 10: Focus on the Patient (Chapter 2)

This transformer is about the need for organizational emphasis on the patient, their family, and how they receive care and services. This includes keeping the impact on the patient at the forefront of the mission and vision of the organization and within all improvement initiatives and day-to-day operations. Organizations must systematically implement policies, programs, and a culture that will address the multiple aspects of patient-centeredness, including respect for patient preferences, needs, and values; the importance of patients' emotional needs and physical and emotional comfort; and shared decision-making as an approach to patient and family engagement. Delivering patient-centered care demands both awareness and responsiveness to the patient experience. It also requires involving patients and family members in committees, strategic initiatives, and improvement efforts.

Transformer 9: Reliably Implement the Basics (Chapter 3)

This transformer is about reliably implementing known best practices. The tried and true healthcare processes in which the evidence has been studied, documented, and proven to be effective in improving the health of patients. This transformer is not about the next great idea, but how to consistently implement, disseminate, and sustain at a high-performance level these practices. A transformed healthcare system will require the consistent implementation of these best practices. A dissemination plan must be in place to effectively spread best practices throughout a health system. As compelling as best practices or improvement results may be, they will not easily transfer to other areas without a formal plan that is designed and monitored to ensure success.

Transformer 8: Value-Based Care (Chapter 4)

This transformer is about emerging payment and delivery models that move away from volume of care, and towards value in care. This requires a system that focuses on data, outcomes, and continual improvement. Payments for performance in care delivery are shifting how organizations view their goals and hold the potential to transform the health of communities. This chapter will summarize different types of pay-for-performance systems currently in place. How to operationalize them and what impact they are having (intentional and unintentional), is a critical transformer to break away from the industry's antiquated payment mechanisms.

Reforming the payment system is not a panacea to improve healthcare; however, it is necessary. The healthcare leader's efforts for payment reform should include four major elements:

1. Assess the current payment system and identify areas where the incentives are misaligned.
2. Evaluate the impact of new payment models on the organization's bottom line.
3. Design and test new payment schemes.
4. Learn from these systems.

Transformer 7: Health Equity (Chapter 5)

Very simply, not everyone experiences the same care, service, and outcomes. This varies greatly based on so many factors – gender, race, ethnicity, language spoken, sexual orientation, and many more – few of which are about actual healthcare needs. These healthcare disparities have been known for decades, however, their awareness has increased in the last several years. They witnessed a true awakening during the pandemic when there were stark realities in the differences in COVID mortality rates by race. Addressing health equity is essential to improving overall healthcare quality and eliminating disparities in care, service, and outcomes. This chapter will address key elements of health equity and critical components of data stratification, unconscious bias, diversity, inclusion, and many other organizational and environmental factors to improve care for all.

Transformer 6: Population Health (Chapter 6)

Research shows that medical care only impacts a person's health status in a minor way – in the range of 20% to 35%. The main factors that drive population outcomes are social determinants of health – factors such as health behaviors, education, economy, and the physical environment. As important as providing great medical care is, it is all the other "life stuff" that truly determines one's health status. Thus, healthcare organizations must address these non-medical care factors to improve population health. This chapter will address those factors and how healthcare delivery organizations can transform population or community health by focusing on the social determinants of health.

Transformer 5: Technology (Chapter 7)

This transformer is about the promise of the impact of technology on better health and healthcare. Although there are a vast number of emerging technologies, including electronic health records, virtual platforms, artificial intelligence, and machine learning systems, how organizations implement and leverage these will determine their success. Yet, more technology is not always better. Those organizations that are forward-thinking and take the time to intentionally implement and strategically utilize technology will be the most successful.

Transformer 4: Transparency (Chapter 8)

This transformer is about the need to transparently share data and information publicly. This includes not only data about quality, outcomes, and costs but also about errors and deficiencies. Transparent organizations seek transformation through quality improvement such as public reporting as well as accountability and trust. Both patients and systems are using data for decision-making and discussion with their providers. In this increasingly competitive healthcare industry, demonstrating excellence and focusing on improvement allows organizations to stand out among peers and competitors.

Transformer 3: Strategy (Chapter 9)

When thinking of Boards, the first thing that often comes to mind is strategy and the concurrent Board role in developing, partnering, and driving it. The measured and constant focus on strategy for the organization is key to the Board's function in oversight and accountability. Strategy links measures and goals with tactics and actions. There are frequently major disruptors in many organization's strategic plans and aspirations, such as was witnessed during the COVID-19 pandemic. However, there must remain continual emphasis on organizational strategy, measures that tie to it, and regular recalibration for the short and long term.

Transformer 2: Culture (Chapter 10)

This transformer is about the culture in an organization and how it defines the ways things are done. This is reflective of the behaviors, norms, and beliefs of team members. Culture is the most often spoken barrier to improving healthcare and yet perhaps the least understood. To create a positive culture that will enhance quality and patient safety, leaders should:

- Make quality and patient safety strategic imperatives.
- Promulgate values of openness of information, a learning organization, and a "no-blame culture."
- Institute policies, systems, and procedures to ensure quick and accurate reporting and discussion of medical errors.

■ Conduct team-building to ensure interdisciplinary collaboration, mutual respect, and effective problem-solving of patient care issues.

Transformer 1: Leadership (Chapter 11)

This transformer reinforces leadership as the underlying key to organizational performance. Leaders must use proven approaches and act to ensure high-quality of care and patient safety. Leaders should set organizational vision and values, maintain accountability, and promote a culture of patient safety. They must initiate *transformational change*, that is, changes in values and patterns of behavior so that healthcare organizations address long-standing performance and quality issues. An excellent framework to follow is IHI's Reinersten's model of transformational leadership, which consists of five interrelated activities:

1. Setting direction (e.g., having a clear mission, vision, and strategy)
2. Establishing a foundation (e.g., developing future leaders)
3. Building will (e.g., defining the business case for quality)
4. Generating ideas (e.g., benchmarking to find best practices)
5. Executing change (e.g., making quality a line responsibility) (Ransom et al. 2008)

Organization of the Book

The format of this book is straightforward. A chapter is devoted to each of the ten healthcare transformers. As mentioned in the preface, the chapters are organized by:

■ The problem: A brief, quantitative look at the problem.
■ The transformer: What will transform and make healthcare different.
■ Best practices: Examples of current best practices indicative of the transformer.
■ Board questions: Questions every board member should consider asking and every healthcare executive should ask and be prepared to answer.

This book is purposefully written to be concise. It is meant to be used as a guide for you to understand context, best practices, and the most important questions to ask in governance.

The concluding chapter provides a compilation of all the board questions for each chapter as an easy-to-use reference for discussion at board meetings.

References

American Academy of Physician Associates (AAP). "The Patient Experience: Perspectives on Today's Healthcare". Poll conducted by Harris Insights & Analytics. Published 2022. Last Accessed January 26, 2024. Available at: https://www.aapa.org/download/113513/?tmstv=1684243672

Auerbach, A.D., Kripalani, S., Vasilevskis, E.E., et al. "Preventability and Causes of Readmissions in a National Cohort of General Medicine Patients". *JAMA Intern Med.* 2016;176(4):484–493.

Callender, A. N., Hastings, D. A., Hemsley, M. C., Morris, L., and Peregrine, M. W. "Corporate Responsibility and Health Care Quality: A Resource for Health Care Boards of Directors". U.S. Department Health and Human Services and American Health Lawyers Association. Published July 18, 2007. Last Accessed February 26, 2024. Available from: http://www.oig.hhs.gov/fraud/docs/complianceguidance/CorporateResponsibilityFinal%209-4-07.pdf

CMS. "CMS (Centers for Medicare & Medicaid Services)". National Health Expenditure Fact Sheet 2023a. Last Accessed January 21, 2024. Available from: https://www.cms.gov/data-research/statistics-trends-and-reports/national-health-expenditure-data/nhe-fact-sheet

CMS. "Hospital Readmissions Reduction Program (HRRP)". Hospital Data from 2023b. Last Accessed January 26, 2024. Available at: https://qualitynet.cms.gov/inpatient/hrrp

CMS. "Hospital Consumer Assessment of Healthcare Providers and Systems: 2023 Percentiles". Posted November 8, 2023c. Last Accessed January 26, 2024. Available at: https://hcahpsonline.org/globalassets/hcahps/summary-analyses/percentiles/2023-10-percentiles-public-report.pdf

Cooper, Z., Stiegman, O., Ndumele, C.D., Staiger, B., and Skinner, J. Geographical Variation in Health Spending Across the US Among Privately Insured Individuals and Enrollees in Medicaid and Medicare. *JAMA Netw Open.* 2022;5(7):e2222138.

Eckel, P., Hill, B., Green, M. On Change: En Route to Transformation. American Council on Education, 1998, http://www.acenet.edu/bookstore/pdf/on-change/on-changeI.pdf. Last Accessed November 10, 2008.

Gunja, M., Gumas, E., Williams, R. "U.S. Health Care from a Global Perspective, 2022: Accelerating Spending, Worsening Outcomes". The Commonwealth Fund, January 31, 2023.

Institute of Medicine Committee on Quality of Health Care in America. *To Err is Human: Building a Safer Health System.* Washington, DC: National Academy Press, 2000.

Kaiser Family Foundation. "American's Challenges with Health Care Costs". Published December 21, 2023. Last Accessed January 26, 2024. Available at: https://www.kff.org/health-costs/issue-brief/americans-challenges-with-health-care-costs/

Leatherman, S., Berwick, D. "Accelerating Global Improvements in Health Care Quality". *JAMA* 2020;324(24):2479–2480.

Lowery, T. "Genetic Code Vs. Zip Code: The Social Determinants of Health". Forbes. Published June 13, 2022. Last Accessed January 26, 2024. Available at:

https://www.forbes.com/sites/forbestechcouncil/2022/06/13/genetic-code-vs-zip-code-the-social-determinants-of-health/?sh=2b548383581c

Payerchin, R. "Appointment Wait Times Drop for Family Physicians, Indicating Shift in Care." Medical Economics. Published September 13, 2022. Last Accessed January 26, 2024. Available at: https://www.medicaleconomics.com/view/appointment-wait-times-drop-for-family-physicians-indicating-shift-in-care

Ransom, E., Joshi, M., Nash, D., and Ransom, S. *The Healthcare Quality Book*, 2nd ed. Chicago: Health Administration Press, 2008.

Schneider, E.C., Shah, A., Doty, M.M., Tikkanen, R., Fields, K., Williams, R.D. "Mirror, Mirror 2021 — Reflecting Poorly: Health Care in the U.S. Compared to Other High-Income Countries" *Commonwealth Fund*. Published August 4, 2021. Last Accessed February 26, 2024. Available at: https://www.commonwealthfund.org/publications/fund-reports/2021/aug/mirror-mirror-2021-reflecting-poorly

Shrank, W.H., Rogstad, T.L., and Parekh, N. Waste in the US Health Care System: Estimated Costs and Potential for Savings. *JAMA*. 2019;322(15):1501–1509.

SteelFischer, G., Findling, M., Caporello, H., Lubell, K., Vidoloff Melville, K., Lane, L., et al. "Trust in US Federal, State, and Local Public Health Agencies During COVID-19: Responses and Policy Implications". *Health Affairs*. 42(3). Published March 2023.

Chapter 2

Healthcare Transformer 10: Focus on the Patient

As the healthcare industry continues to grow, with new team members and emerging technologies, it is easy to lose sight of the ultimate goal. That is, taking good care of each patient, their needs, their health, and their illnesses. Without patients and without illness there would be little necessity for a system of care in the first place. Thus, all organizations must seek to place the patient first and to ensure that the focus surrounding all efforts remains on and about the patient.

There are multiple definitions and models of patient-centered care, which has also been characterized as person-centered, family-centered, relationship-centered, consumer-focused, and consumer-directed. However, throughout these various descriptions of patient-centeredness, the American Board of Internal Medicine Foundation has identified common themes:

- Respect for patients' preferences, needs, and values.
- Importance of patients' emotional needs and physical and emotional comfort.
- Engagement and dialogue with patients by asking about their needs, listening to their concerns, empathizing, and providing information.
- Incorporation of shared decision-making and promotion of patient autonomy, while also involving family and friends in care decisions when appropriate.

DOI: 10.4324/9781003493914-2

- A more holistic view of healthcare by stressing the incorporation of features such as music, art, spiritual issues, and complementary medicine.
- A reflective clinician who is aware of how his or her emotions and experiences may affect practice.
- Focus on care coordination and continuity over time and within and across care settings (Cunningham 2008).

Regardless of the nuances of different definitions, caring for patients and focusing on their needs are at the heart of the healthcare profession and for many is the reason that they selected healthcare as their vocation. However, the healthcare system is fraught with dysfunctional systems of care and poor service in which patient-centeredness is not the driving factor. Compared with the ideal, healthcare falls dramatically short in the actual practice of patient-centeredness.

This chapter on the first transformer, Focus on the Patient offers practical and meaningful strategies and tactics for care design and redesign in which the patient and family are placed at the center (Figure 2.1). The placement of the patient at the top of the ten transformers as depicted in a larger overriding bubble in the graphic is intentional, as health system leaders and all team members should keep this focus at the top of all that they do.

Problem

Several problems are associated with the lack of patient- and family-centeredness. The first is the number of distractions that have increasingly entered the healthcare delivery space, pulling time and focus away from the patient as the central element of care. Even when patients are figuratively at that center, the number of team members, technologies, and organizational silos that have arisen have impacted the ability of patients to feel a sense of centeredness. The following studies suggest the dramatic level of distraction and interruption away from "eyes on the patient" in contemporary healthcare:

- Clinicians have been shown to interrupt a patient after a median of just 11 seconds. Further, when not interrupted, patients take just around 6 seconds to state their concerns (Singh Ospina et al. 2019).
- One study of ambulatory care in four different specialties showed the average doctor spends just 27% of their day face-to-face with patients. Meanwhile, 49.2% of their time is spent in the electronic health record and doing other administrative tasks. The study showed that doctors spend

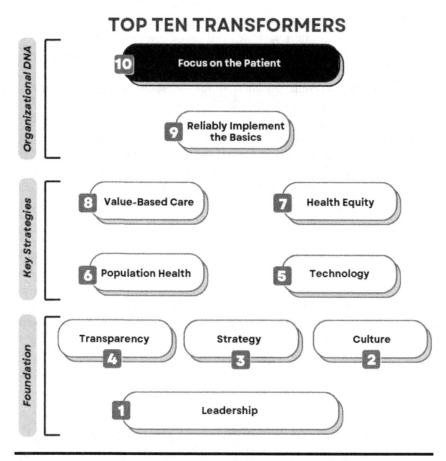

Figure 2.1   Top ten healthcare transformers.

2 hours on administrative tasks, such as documentation, for every 1 hour of face-to-face time with patients (Sinsky et al. 2016).

◼ The average medical intern physician spends over 66% of their working day away from the bedside, performing tasks that are indirect to patient care. Effectively, for every 24 hours of their work, less than 5 hours are spent with patients – 3 hours in direct patient care and 1.8 hours in patient education (Chaiyachati et al. 2019).

To improve these circumstances, it is critical to have accurate and reliable input from patients and families on their healthcare experiences. With the emergence of the Consumer Assessment of Healthcare Providers and Systems (CAHPS) Hospital Survey, such input is now more readily and frequently available because it is based on the use of a well-researched survey instrument utilized throughout all hospitals in the country. This allows comparison between similar organizations, as well as internal benchmarking and trending. However, surveys alone do not always provide a complete picture or actionable opportunity of how a patient and their family members feel about the customer service and medical care they receive. Thus, major challenges continue for organizations in how they receive and solicit input from their customers as well as translate that input into action.

There are many barriers inherent in recognizing and responding to patients' perceptions of hospital care. Data from 2023 from more than 4400 hospitals nationwide demonstrated that overall only 69% of patients would definitely recommend the hospital in which they received care. Incredibly, this number has increased by just 1% over the past 15 years, up from 68% of patients positive in the recommendation of their hospital in 2007 (CMS 2023, 2008). Are hospitals not adapting or seeking change? Are patients more critical in their response? Have expectations changed? Are we asking the right questions? The answer is likely a mix of each of these and more. However, it underlies the simultaneous challenge and the necessity inherent in understanding patient experience.

Patient experience scores for individual dimensions are also variable and low. The United States average for the quietness of the room and the hospital environment is 62%, communication about medicines is 62%, and responsiveness of hospital staff is 66%. Is it possible that 1 out of 3 patients leaves the hospital not feeling that their experience in these areas was positive? Post-hospital surveys suggest as much.

Building on these two problems, there is a legal and financial impact associated with services that are not patient-centered and result in low patient satisfaction. Numerous studies have shown that the relationship and communication between the patient and the physician, nurse, and staff are significant predictors of complaints, risks, and malpractice claims. The research has shown that:

■ The most common cause of malpractice suits is failed communication with patients and their families, with communication failures identified in a staggering 49% of claims. Claims with communication failures were significantly less likely to be dropped, denied, or dismissed than claims without (Humphrey et al. 2022).
■ Patient-centered communication skills are associated with improved health outcomes (Sharkiya 2023).

Patient experience and satisfaction as one defined aspect of patient-centeredness has a dramatic impact on the performance of an organization in many realms— clinical quality, service, and financial.

To become more patient-centered means fundamentally changing the culture, policies, and practices of organizations. These changes should seek the treatment of patients with dignity, respect, and awareness of who they are and where they come from. It is the simplicity inherent in the golden rule, that is so frequently misplaced – treat others as you would be treated. A good place to start is to imagine the kind of care that you would want for yourself, a family member, or a friend – then ask the question – "Does my organization routinely deliver and expect that this happens for every patient?"

Transformer

Although practically few individuals would be opposed to the idea of patient-centeredness, the reality is that the healthcare industry has not reliably and systematically changed systems so that service and care are focused on patient and family needs. Figure 2.2 displays a roadmap for a six-step plan to assess, identify, test, and evaluate patient-centered approaches.

1. Perform organizational self-assessment: Through conducting a self-assessment, the organization will better understand its strengths and weaknesses compared with best practices. Examples of tools available to conduct

Figure 2.2 Patient-centeredness implementation roadmap.

an assessment include the *Patient- and Family-Centered Care Organizational Self-Assessment Tool* from IHI and the National Initiative for Children's Healthcare Quality (IHI 2013) *Patient- and Family-Centered Care Hospital Self-Assessment Inventory* (IPFCC 2017). Although the assessment instruments differ in their questions, they generally cover similar major dimensions, such as leadership, mission and values, quality improvement, personnel, information and education, design of the environment, medical charting and documentation, and care support. It is important to obtain multiple perspectives in completing the self-assessment, including those from senior leaders, frontline staff, and patients and families.

2. Review findings: A team should review the self-assessment findings, noting the strengths and weaknesses according to the major dimensions of patient-centeredness.

3. Prioritize improvement opportunities: Using the self-assessment findings, it is critical to prioritize the improvement plans. Resource constraints, largest potential gains, and importance to the mission and strategy of the organization should be considered.

4. Implement interventions: Implementation is where the most challenges occur. Implementing interventions requires a disciplined and well-planned improvement project with measurable aims, accountabilities, deadlines, detailed steps, and monitoring. All of these elements are essential to having an improvement project plan with a high yield of success. Emerging interventions that are proving to make significant patient-centered gains include:

■ Involving patients and families in improvement teams, advisory councils, and task forces

■ Sharing patient stories of medical errors and near misses with leadership and governance

■ Ensuring that patients and families are part of hospital leadership walking rounds

■ Making patients and families an important part of multidisciplinary daily rounds

■ Instituting open and flexible visiting policies on all patient units

■ Providing patients and their identified family members immediate and transparent access to all of their medical records

■ Empowering patients with the ability to update and add to their health history and records

■ Creating open and bidirectional lines of communication in which patients have access and communication with their healthcare teams

■ Designing educational materials that are appropriate for the patient population in readability and language

- Offering translation services
- Offering accommodations for disabilities and barriers to care
- Ensure patient-centered approaches to care encounters, change-of-shift reports, and patient education

5. Measure and evaluate changes: Clear measures and goals for the improvement projects are necessary to make sure projects are achieving intended outcomes or for modifying and testing new interventions if needed.
6. Conduct periodic reassessment: The organization annually, or with intentional frequency, completes a self-assessment to provide a milestone progress report.

This continuous improvement process ensures that interventions are purposely planned, implemented, tested, evaluated, and improved.

Best Practices

In his 2009 book, Simon Sinek encouraged all leaders to "Start with Why". Most organizations tend to focus on "what" they do, and some good organizations will be able to speak to "how" they go about doing it. For Sinek, truly great organizations can clearly articulate not only a mission and vision but also "why" they exist (Sinek 2011). In healthcare, this is the very essence of putting the patient first and focusing on their individual circumstances and needs. Much of healthcare is "done to" patients as opposed to "done for" them. To truly understand the best way to treat and care for patients, it is essential to understand what they want out of life, and what matters most to them in their health. This allows the opportunity to provide care that aligns with an individual's life goals.

What Matters

One model for patient-centered care is the Age-Friendly Health System, developed by IHI, AHA, and the John A. Hartford Foundation. This offers simple guidance for an essential set of evidence-based practices that organize care for older adults. Among these are identifying "what matters" for every patient. This is the knowledge and alignment of care with each older adult's specific health outcome goals and care preferences, including, but not limited to, end-of-life care, and across settings of care (IHI 2018). Some health systems are asking all their patients "what matters" and it is being recorded in their electronic medical record. It can then be used as a conversation and relationship building between the patient, the providers, and the staff.

Meritus Health System has integrated "What Matters" as a prominent aspect of care both inside and outside of the hospital. Not only are all patients asked what matters to them, but their answers are highlighted as a key and visible element of their patient chart – depicted just below their name and date of birth. This means that all team members, from front desk staff to clinicians, can see the things that matter to patients in their own words. Consider the impact of the initiative from the following patient examples:

- For one patient in the hospital near the end of life what mattered to him was seeing his daughter get married. The hospital nurses rallied the organization, which included decorations and the setup of a service in the hospital chapel. Nutrition services even made a wedding cake. The ceremony was held and the family was forever grateful.
- For a 9-year-old girl what mattered to her was time with her cat Bingo. Even though this may not seem connected to her health at face value, the fact that her love for her cat was listed prominently on her chart allowed all team members to know and have the chance to ask her about Bingo. For an otherwise timid child, this provided the unique opportunity to make immediate connections, and her face would light up with a big smile every time she was asked.
- For a 68-year-old woman what mattered most was tending to her garden. This information allowed her primary care team to help maximize her ability to do so, treating her allergies and knee pain to support her mobility just in time for each spring planting season.

In these instances, and countless more, knowing what mattered to the patient was patient-centered care.

Patient and Family Advisory Councils (PFACs)

Patient and family engagement (PFE) is a key element for organizations that deliver safe, high-quality, patient-centered care. Patient and Family Advisory Councils (PFACs) should be developed to help provide feedback and engagement on care delivery transformations. These are freestanding committees that provide patients the opportunity for input on organizational operations, policy, and processes. As an advisory panel, PFACs provide timely, valuable, and real-world feedback on challenges as well as new ideas from the patient perspective. Organizations not only stand to learn but also to demonstrate responsiveness and potentially strengthen patient and community relationships. There are additional benefits to be gained from new insights that can improve care processes and develop stronger relationships. Studies have shown that organizations that support PFACs have increased employee satisfaction and improved financial performance (AHRQ 2024).

The culture of focusing on the patient first must be reinforced by senior leadership and throughout the entire organization. It must go beyond just the face-to-face episodes of care but must be embedded within the fabric of how all team members see their work. For instance, members of a finance team should consider that, even if they never directly care for a patient, their efforts have tremendous benefits on how patients are ultimately cared for. Members of facilities, environmental services, and countless other non-clinical teams will inevitably still interact with and cross paths with patients and families regularly. A patient-first mindset will greatly impact the impression and sense of a caring environment. Extending from the system level, specific clinical areas should emphasize how their units can be more patient-focused.

These few best practices highlight the dramatic impact on financial and patient outcomes that the implementation of patient-centered programs can have as culture changes and new practices are put in place.

Board Questions

As a health system board member, consider these questions:

1. Does our organization deliver care to every patient in the way I would want for myself, a family member, or a friend?
2. What are our biggest gaps and improvement opportunities in patient-centeredness?
3. How are patients and families involved in the design of our improvement efforts?
4. How are patients and families engaged in their care?
5. Are there evidenced-based patient-centered interventions that we should try implementing; for example, sharing patient stories of medical errors and near misses at leadership and board meetings, providing apologies, disclosing errors, including patients on improvement teams, and cultivating patient and family advisory councils?

References

AHRQ. Working with Patient and Families as Advisors: Implementation Handbook. Last Accessed February 26, 2024. Available at: https://www.ahrq.gov/sites/default/files/wysiwyg/professionals/systems/hospital/engagingfamilies/strategy1/Strat1_Implement_Hndbook_508_v2.pdf

Centers for Medicare and Medicaid Services (CMS). *Summary of HCAHPS Survey Results.* Baltimore: CMS, 2008.

Centers for Medicare and Medicaid Services (CMS). Summary of HCAHPS Survey Results. Baltimore: CMS: April 2022 to March 2023 Discharges. Baltimore, MD. Last accessed January 31, 2024. Available at: https://www.hcahpsonline.org/globalassets/hcahps/summary-analyses/summary-results/january-2024-public-report-april-2022---march-2023.pdf

Chaiyachati, K.H., Shea, J.A., Asch, D.A., et al. "Assessment of Inpatient Time Allocation among First-Year Internal Medicine Residents Using Time-Motion Observations". *JAMA Intern Med.* 2019;179(6):760–767.

Cunningham, A. "Synthesis of Definitions of Patient-, Family- and Relationship-Centered Care". Presented at the ABIM Foundation 2008 Forum, July 26–29, 2008, in Yountville Napa Valley, CA.

Humphrey, K.E., Sundberg, M., Milliren, C.E., Graham, D.A., Landrigan, C.P. "Frequency and Nature of Communication and Handoff Failures in Medical Malpractice Claims". *J Patient Saf.* 2022 Mar 1;18(2):130–137.

Institute for Family-Centered Care. Advancing the Practice of Patient- and Family- Centered Care in Hospitals: How to Get Started. Published January 2017. Last Accessed February 26, 2024. Available at: https://www.ipfcc.org/resources/GettingStarted-AmbulatoryCare.pdf

Institute for Healthcare Improvement (IHI) and National Initiative for Children's Healthcare Quality. Patient- and Family-Centered Care Organizational Self-Assessment Tool. Published June 2013. Last Accessed January 31, 2024. Available at: https://nichq.org/sites/default/files/resource-file/Patient_and_family_centered_care_organizational_self-assessment_tool.pdf

Institute for Healthcare Improvement (IHI). The Business Case for Becoming and Age-Friendly Health System. Published 2018. Last Accessed January 31, 2024. Available at: https://www.ihi.org/sites/default/files/2023-09/IHI_Business_Case_for_Becoming_Age_Friendly_Health_System.pdf

Sharkiya, S.H. "Quality Communication Can Improve Patient-Centred Health Outcomes among Older Patients: A Rapid Review". *BMC Health Serv Res* 2023;23:886.

Singh Ospina, N., Phillips, K.A., Rodriguez-Gutierrez, R., Castaneda-Guarderas, A., Gionfriddo, M.R., Branda, M.E., Montori, V.M. "Eliciting the Patient's Agenda-Secondary Analysis of Recorded Clinical Encounters". *J Gen Intern Med.* 2019 Jan;34(1):36–40.

Sinek, S. *Start with Why.* Penguin Books, Harlow, England, 2011.

Sinsky, C., Colligan, L., Li, L., Prgomet, M., Reynolds, S., Goeders, L., et al. "Allocation of Physician Time in Ambulatory Practice: A Time and Motion Study in 4 Specialties". *Ann Intern Med.* 2016 Dec 6;165(11):753–760.

Chapter 3

Healthcare Transformer 9: Reliably Implement the Basics

Healthcare Transformer 3 (see Figure 3.1) has little to do with innovation in terms of new medical science. Rather, this transformer is about reliably implementing the basics, that is the tried-and-true best practices of care delivery. If you accept tried and true to mean "tested and proven to be worthy," there are numerous healthcare practices that are tried and true, but not consistently done for every patient every day in the American healthcare system.

The gap between current healthcare and the ideal of best care is significant and persistent. Thus, achieving higher levels of performance is not a trivial matter. Often, individuals and organizations try to lead by producing outside-the-box thinking, innovation, or novel technology. However, this transformer is not about the next great idea, but how we can consistently implement, at a high-performance level, practices that have been thoroughly well-researched and for which the evidence has been known for years. A transformed healthcare system requires a commitment to quality improvement as well as the consistent implementation, dissemination, and sustainment of best practices. These are the basics that successful organizations rely upon to propel their strategic plans, initiatives, growth, and excellence.

 DOI: 10.4324/9781003493914-3

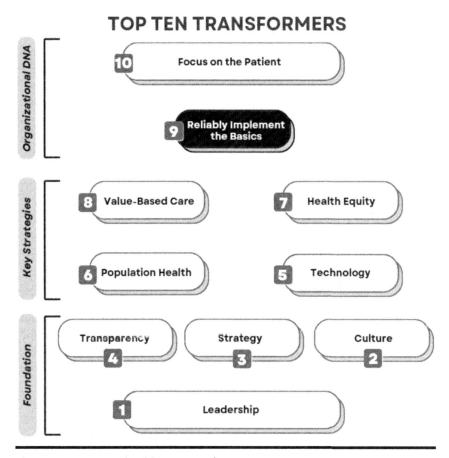

Figure 3.1   Top ten healthcare transformers.

Problem

The field of health care has longstanding challenges that have limited the translation of research and science into day-to-day practice. Some of this has to do with inconsistent or insufficient financial incentives to compel change. But much of this comes down to the silos and distance that exist between those institutions that develop best practices, and those that are accountable to deploy them. In addition, staffing changes, lack of oversight and accountability, limited reporting mechanisms, and communication all impact the consistent application of basics and best practices. Consider the following data:

- 64%: This is the national average for the percentage of surgery patients (for certain surgeries) who received preventive antibiotic(s) as recommended before or during surgery. Research shows that surgery patients who get timely antibiotics, typically within the hour before their operation, are less likely to get wound infections. Such infections lead to 1 million excess days spent in the hospital and $1.6 billion in health care costs each year, yet it is estimated that half of these are preventable (Bardia et al. 2021). The primary literature and initial publication of practice guidelines for antibiotic prescribing before surgery were released in 1999, with major updates in 2010. (Bratzler et al. 2013). Despite this, one in every 3 surgery patients today still do not get the right antibiotic at the right time.
- 50%: This is the national estimated average for appropriate hand hygiene, including the cleaning and washing of hands, by all healthcare providers during the care of patients (Makhni et al. 2021). Research demonstrating the effectiveness of hand washing has been available since the 1860s, and the first CDC guideline was published in 1981 (Larson et al. 2007). This data is challenging to measure, but the best studies have identified high-performing institutions with rates in the 90% for all in-hospital care. That means that if you are a patient at even the best hospitals in the country for this measure of quality, 1 out of every 10 times a team member cares for you, they may not appropriately wash their hands before seeing you.
- 17 years: This is the estimate for the amount of time on average, it takes for a research finding to be adopted as a health intervention. While this gap sounds staggering, it is perhaps worse to consider that only 1 in 5 evidence-based interventions ever even make it to routine clinical practice (Rubin 2023).

It is the magnitude of these numbers that is grave to healthcare leaders. The time it takes for important learning to become common practice is substantial, and this problem is heightened by the fact that patients' lives and health are at stake. The results are far from 100%. However, for many such goals, 100% may be theoretical and difficult to achieve. Even if one considers 99% or 95% as the goal, these results are a stark deviation from the best. The benefits of improving these types of healthcare processes include financial savings and human savings in the form of reduced cost, reduced complications, reduced deaths, better quality of life, and greater patient and provider satisfaction.

Dr. Ken Kizer, former president and chief executive officer of the National Quality Forum and former Undersecretary for Health in the U.S. Department of Veterans Affairs, stated:

If we would systematically apply what we currently know about quality management to healthcare, it has the potential to save more lives and otherwise improve health more than any foreseeable technological or scientific breakthrough of the next 20 years, including finding cures for diabetes, heart disease, or cancer.

("The Face of Quality" 2005)

Transformer

The transformative opportunity to reliably implement and disseminate tried-and-true practices is multifold and includes:

1. Quality improvement vision and approach: The organization must set forth its quality improvement goals, philosophy, and process improvement model. All three are vital topics for inclusion in any training or development effort.
2. Measurable aims: It is critical for improvement to have clear, measurable aims and goals that specifically include the measures to be tracked, the goals to be achieved, and the dates for meeting goals. The aims provide the milestones to work toward.
3. Track results: Constant surveillance of key healthcare process results should take place at the management and governance levels. Key results should be reviewed at least quarterly and actionable so that one can assess the impact of a test of change. For those directly involved in the process, monthly, weekly, or even daily reviews should be commonplace.
4. Project review: Senior leadership should establish a system for ongoing review of key quality improvement initiatives. Assessment should include progress made as well as how barriers can be removed and enablers created.
5. Implementation: Effectively implementing interventions is a challenge in every hospital. Implementation includes many types of interventions that need to be delivered in multiple ways.
6. Program evaluation and reinforcement: The organization must continually evaluate the effectiveness of its development efforts, continually assess if new knowledge or experience is needed, and provide reinforcement and continuing education as needed.

One set of interventions includes training and education. Continuous training and education of all staff and providers on current and emerging best practices is essential, whether as a formal program or just-in-time training. This should be repeated with enough frequency such that new staff members are engaged and all others remain engaged. While implementation and dissemination are challenging, sustainment of best practices can be equally challenging. Incentives, financial and non-financial, can also play a role in encouraging and rewarding improvement. The evidence is clear that incentives for staff and clinicians on performance accelerates improvement. Finally, there exists a core of high-reliability concepts, and the implementation of these concepts yields better performance. High-reliability concepts include being sensitive to operations, reluctant to simplify explanations to problems, preoccupied with failure, resilient to quickly respond to errors, and deferent to frontline expertise (Agency for Healthcare Research and Quality 2008).

Specific to the last point, several interventions are available that can make processes more reliable. The interventions include education, training, development, and implementation of standardized protocols, checklists, and bundles of care.

Whether it is called knowledge transfer, translating research into practice, spreading improvement, diffusion of innovations, or disseminating best practices, the process and structure of taking something that works well from one part of the system to the rest of the system is no easy task, and it does not happen organically.

To effectively disseminate best practices throughout a health system, it is essential to have a dissemination plan in place. Trying to convince everyone of the need for change will not achieve the desired result. Rather, organizations should recognize the five stages of the adoption of a change (Rogers 1995):

1. Awareness
2. Interest
3. Evaluation
4. Trial
5. Adoption

Regardless of the model or framework used, the most important piece is having a plan in place that is designed upfront with clear, measurable goals; is driven by leadership; considers all of the important environmental and social factors that prevent and enable progress; and is monitored and improved for ongoing success.

Best Practices

There are numerous examples of best practices for the previously mentioned and other important clinical areas. These best practices are found in every type of hospital—small and large, teaching and non-teaching, as well as those urban and rural.

Evidence-Based Recommendations

Interventions that can dramatically improve the quality of healthcare include:

- Standing orders and clinical guidelines: Standing orders are a course of treatments and tests that each patient with a given clinical situation receives unless a physician believes there is a compelling reason to change or augment the order. Each instruction requires staff members treating the patient to document what action they took, including any decision not to follow the recommendations. Clinical guidelines are similar in that they are standardized approaches to treating conditions for which the evidence is clear for the best approach.

- Checklists: As simple as it sounds, using a checklist to ensure that all of a patient's individual care practices have been completed has proven to be incredibly effective for health care improvement. Checklists are simple in form, serve as a prompt and effective reminder, require less reliance on memory, and can be put into practice efficiently. For example, a checklist to prevent bloodstream infections would include: performing standard hand disinfection before any procedure, wearing a mask, using a sterile gown and gloves, and preparing the site with a chlorhexidine stick.

- Care bundles: Care bundles are groupings of best practices concerning a disease process that individually improve care, but when applied together result in substantially greater improvement. The science supporting the bundle components is considered the standard of care.

- Debriefs: When deviation from the expected care process or outcomes occurs, involved teams and team members should meet to discuss what occurred. This allows review and discussion of performance or error without judgment. Debriefing is performed to integrate learnings and improvement and prevent issues from reoccurring.

Board Questions

As a health system board member, consider these questions:

1. How are we doing in implementing and disseminating tried-and-true best practices?
2. How do our results compare to, not only to state and national averages but to benchmarks – such as the top decile or quartile?

3. Have we learned from the best-performing organizations that have achieved benchmark performance?
4. What are the major lessons (successes and failures) from our recent quality improvement initiatives?
5. What are our biggest barriers to the adoption of best practices, and what specific strategies are we using to overcome those barriers?
6. Is quality improvement a necessary competency for professional advancement and for leadership?

References

Agency for Healthcare Research and Quality (AHRQ). Becoming a High-Reliability Organization: Operational Advice for Hospital Leaders. AHRQ Publication No. 08-0022. Rockville, MD: AHRQ. Published April 9, 2008. Last Accessed February 26, 2024. Available at: https://archive.ahrq.gov/professionals/quality-patient-safety/quality-resources/tools/hroadvice/hroadvice.pdf

Bardia, A., Treggiari, M.M., Michel, G., et al. "Adherence to Guidelines for the Administration of Intraoperative Antibiotics in a Nationwide US Sample". *JAMA Netw Open.* 2021;4(12):e2137296.

Bratzler, D.W., Dellinger, E.P., Olsen, K.M., et al. "Clinical Practice Guidelines for Antimicrobial Prophylaxis in Surgery". *Am J Health-Syst Pharm.* 2013; 70:195–283.

Kizer, K. "The Face of Quality." *Quality Progress.* January 22, 2005.

Larson, E.L., Quiros, D., Lin, S.X. "Dissemination of the CDC's Hand Hygiene Guideline and Impact on Infection Rates". *Am J Infect Control.* 2007 Dec;35(10):666–675.

Makhni, S., Umscheid, C.A., Soo, J., Chu, V., Bartlett, A., Landon, E., Marrs, R. "Hand Hygiene Compliance Rate during the COVID-19 Pandemic". *JAMA Intern Med.* 2021 Jul 1;181(7):1006–1008.

Rogers, E. M. *Diffusion of Innovations,* 4th ed. New York: The Free Press, 1995.

Rubin, R. "It Takes an Average of 17 Years for Evidence to Change Practice—the Burgeoning Field of Implementation Science Seeks to Speed Things Up". *JAMA.* 2023;329(16):1333–1336.

Chapter 4

Healthcare Transformer 8: Value-Based Care

Healthcare has traditionally been delivered in a transactional way, with payment provided as services are rendered. The major problem is that such fee-for-service care does not reward better care, or even promote good care at all. Rather, this model of volume-based care encourages doing more – more testing and more treatment to generate more revenue. In recent years, provider and hospital reimbursement in the U.S. healthcare system has begun recognizing and paying for value. This includes new and alternative payment mechanisms that shift the emphasis towards quality and outcomes. Those organizations that can demonstrate lower costs and better care stand to be more successful in the healthcare delivery system of the future.

In this chapter, Healthcare Transformer 8 (Figure 4.1) focuses on providing value in healthcare delivery, in other words, offering the highest quality care at the lowest cost.

Problem

Healthcare in the United States is far costlier than essentially every other industrialized nation in the world. Yet, when compared to those less expensive healthcare systems elsewhere, the US ranks lower both in terms of quality and outcomes.

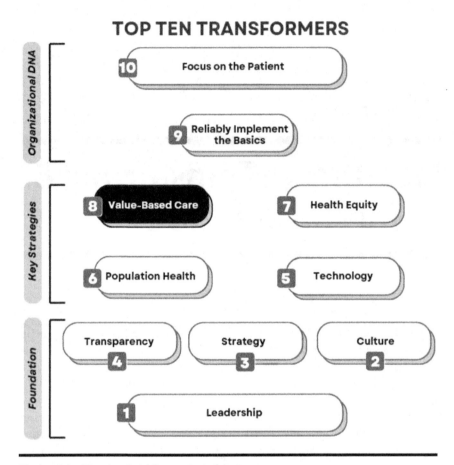

Figure 4.1 Top ten healthcare transformers.

Perhaps worse, the nation is moving in the wrong direction. Recent estimates project that, if unchecked, healthcare spending as a share of GDP will increase by 47% between 2023 and 2052 (GAO 2024). Meanwhile, those born in the United States have a life expectancy of approximately 77.5 years, while the average life expectancy for all other comparable countries is 82.2 years. Even before the COVID-19 pandemic, life expectancy in the United States was decreasing at a rate vastly worse than in similar nations (Kaiser 2024).

Increasingly, Americans have more skin in the game when it comes to the financial implications of healthcare, as employers have started to shift costs to their employees through higher deductible plans and increased premiums (Claxton et al. 2022). A fundamental key driver for these unsustainable costs has been the traditional fee-for-service reimbursement model in which hospitals and physicians are paid by the number of tests, services, and procedures regardless of value. While paying for quality and outcomes has been discussed for decades, in today's healthcare system well over half of all payments are still based entirely on fee-for-service (Health Affairs 2022).

Transformer

Determining value in healthcare delivery can be broken down as simply as in the equation demonstrated in Figure 4.2. That is, that the value of healthcare services is related to the ratio of the quality and cost of those services. Improved value can be produced with higher quality and outcomes as well as lower costs. Conversely, anything that increases the cost of care or reduces the level of quality will lead to a diminished value. Under this equation, it is easy to see why the fee-for-service or volume-based care model is counterproductive for improving health. Many variables can be added to this equation, such as patient or provider experience. However, as a board member, one of the first and easiest ways that you can check if your organization is providing value is to hone in on quality metrics and your costs of care.

Several value-based payment methodologies have emerged to incentivize the transition away from fee-for-service and toward the delivery of high-quality care. The common theme is to reward fewer tests and procedures in the search for care that is necessary, appropriate, timely, and cost-effective. Here are some examples of common value-based payment frameworks:

- **Accountable Care Organizations (ACO):** A hospital or physician group can take the responsibility for caring for a defined group of patients. Healthcare providers may earn more or avoid penalties if they reduce or maintain costs. Thus, if providers can reduce unnecessary use of high-cost forms of care like emergency department visits and inpatient admissions, they may share some of the savings they produce. Some models involve

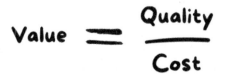

$$Value = \frac{Quality}{Cost}$$

Figure 4.2   Value equation in health care.

greater risk, in which providers or hospitals lose money if spending exceeds targets. Some organizations have chosen to partner together to develop new entities to coordinate care across stakeholders including retail pharmacies, skilled nursing facilities, home health care, and others.

■ **Episode or Bundle-Based Payment:** A single payment for all services needed to care for a specific medical issue over a given time. This could be for all of the costs of a knee replacement or all of the elements of caring for a patient with diabetes for a year. If better value care yields lower costs, then the hospital or group can keep the difference. This encourages enhancing how care is delivered, such as adding care coordination or reducing inefficiencies and redundancies. As an example, for a knee surgery replacement, the bundled payment would include coverage for all inpatient, ambulatory, and postoperative care costs for the procedure as well as the 90 days following the end of surgery.

■ **Pay for Performance (P4P):** Reimbursements are tied directly to metric-driven outcomes, best practices, patient satisfaction, and other markers of quality. Thus, a provider or hospital that provides higher quality care gains higher reimbursement. This can occur even when less is done, for instance, if there are fewer hospital readmissions, emergency room visits, or diabetic patients managed on dialysis. There are both positive and negative attributable performance implications, and in some instances, money is withheld or penalties are imposed for poor quality.

■ **Per Member Per Month (PMPM):** Payments are provided upfront for a given population, regardless of services rendered. Essentially a form of capitated payment, this includes upfront money to proactively address healthcare issues, as opposed to waiting for patients to be ill and present for a documented and billable service. Thus, a clinic may receive $5 every month for every diabetic patient they care for, regardless of whether they are seen for an office visit or not.

Updates in health insurance benefit design have started to shift patient incentives to steer, or even require, care from a high-value provider. Health plans may tier providers based on their cost and quality relative to other similar providers who treat comparable patients. One study showed such a tiered approach decreased total healthcare spending by 5% per member per quarter (Sinaiko, Landrum & Chernew 2017).

These efforts are not going away, as CMS aims to have all Medicare beneficiaries and most Medicaid beneficiaries enrolled in accountable care programs by 2030 (Commonwealth 2023). The transition from volume to value is a key driver of rapid transformation. Those who do not transform quickly enough to produce value through more efficient care processes will no longer flourish.

Best Practices

Delivering value in care can be driven by financial incentives, flexible payment options, and investment in tools to support care management. Organizations must be savvy to understand which of these levers to pull and when to pull them to inspire value in their systems. Consider the following case studies on organizational efforts to improve quality and reduce costs:

The Next Generation Accountable Care Organization (NGACO)

This model evaluated the performance of over 91,000 participating providers caring for 4.2 million beneficiaries across 6 years. This included ACOs with two-sided financial risk and prospective population-based payment models. As improvements in infrastructure and clinical processes occurred, spending reductions grew larger year over year. Ultimately, gross spending declined by 1.9% or 270 dollars per beneficiary per year. Several population health management strategies were associated with spending reductions without reductions in quality of care:

- Embed care management in the inpatient hospital settings
- Identify gaps in care, educate beneficiaries, and foster shared-decision making
- Track beneficiaries at risk for readmission and identify gaps in care
- Prioritize strategies that provide the primary care team with real-time data on beneficiary hospitalization

No single payment, pathway, or structure was shown to be most influential on spending, but rather combinations of factors were found to be more impactful. Organizations should thus consider how to develop and deploy multiple population health management strategies (see chapter 6 for more on this Healthcare Transformer). Meanwhile, larger declines in spending were associated with physician practice affiliation, higher levels of risk, and population-based payment mechanisms (NORC 2024).

Choosing Wisely

Every year in the United States over 5 billion tests are performed in healthcare. Yet, it is thought that upwards of 40–60% of these may be unnecessary and cost the US healthcare system over $100 billion annually (Koch et al. 2018; Shrank et al. 2019). There are a variety of reasons for this, including ease of ordering, patient preference, heuristic bias, fear of liability, and difficulty accessing previous medical records. In response, beginning in 2012 the American Board of Internal

Medicine (ABIM) Foundation developed the Choosing Wisely® Campaign to promote evidence-based care that is not duplicative, free from harm, and truly necessary. The effort includes references and recommendations on whether tests and procedures are appropriate in given circumstances and patient populations. The initiative also developed patient-friendly materials that use straightforward language to inform patients on a host of medical issues, as well as resources to improve physician-patient communication.

Choosing Wisely has engaged over 80 medical specialty organizations and published over 600 recommendations for overused tests and treatments (ABIM Foundation). The goal is for both physicians and patients to question and discuss the necessity of any of these tests. Organizations need to be prepared to highlight the lessons from Chapter 3 on implementing best practices to drive improvement of value through lower costs.

The Value of Doing Less: The Meritus Health team used the Choosing Wisely recommendations as a foundation for reducing unnecessary utilization – that is the ordering of laboratory tests and images (ABIM Foundation n.d.). Their "Doing Wisely" initiative began with support and investment at the system-level from senior leadership, and this cascaded across multiple areas of care delivery. Task forces were established for each of the areas of focus, including daily and routine lab orders in the intensive care unit and hospital floors, day-of-discharge lab orders, preoperative lab testing, and imaging performed in the emergency department. Task force team members were drawn from across the spectrum of care delivery, including physicians, nurses, quality-improvement specialists, radiology leadership, and at times even radiology and laboratory technicians. Each strategy was linked to a physician champion who was accountable for review and progress alongside both oversight and tracking of data. Data was updated and reviewed daily, allowing physicians to review their ordering tendencies down to the level of the individual test, day, and where it was ordered. Physicians were able to see how often they ordered given tests and compare this to their peers.

Ongoing education and training were directed to providers on appropriate use criteria, clinical guidelines, and the risks and benefits of different tests and treatments.

After implementing the Doing Wisely initiative, Meritus Health was able to reduce more than 30,000 unnecessary tests for the year when compared with the previous year. To put this in real terms, there were 2,000 fewer CT scans performed in the Emergency Department compared to the previous year, without any noted changes in patient outcomes. Figure 4.3 depicts the trend and improvement for laboratory and imaging ordering including six months before the start.

These value-based strategies are built upon the recognition that lowering costs and improving quality will lead to better healthcare and outcomes. Organizations

Avg # Lab Orders per Encounter

Avg # ED Imaging Orders per ED Arrival

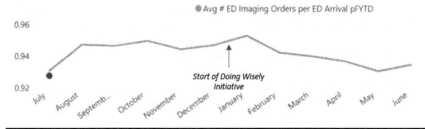

Figure 4.3   Lab and imaging reduction trends at meritus health (Meritus Health, Hagerstown, MD).

must be prepared to shift from traditional practices to best practices and reorient away from the volume of care delivered toward the value inherent within their services.

Board Questions

As a health system board member, consider these questions:

1. How does our organization measure value in our care delivery?
2. What is our organization doing to lower costs?
3. What is the extent of fee-for-service care that your organization participates in?
4. What are the (financial and non-financial) incentives for our clinicians to provide high-quality care?
5. Are there any new value-based care arrangements that we should consider with partners or health plans?
6. What gaps or opportunities exist in our current performance that are limiting higher-value health care delivery?

References

ABIM Foundation. "Choosing Wisely: An Initiative of the ABIM Foundation." n.d. Accessed March 3, 2024. Available at: http://www.choosingwisely.org

Centers for Medicare and Medicaid Services. National Health Expenditure Projections 2021-2030: Forecast Summary. 2021. https://www.cms.gov/Research-Statistics-Data-and-Systems/Statistics-Trends-and-Reports/NationalHealthExpendData

CMS. "Person-Centered Innovation – An Update on the Implementation of the CMS Innovation Center's Strategy". November 2022. Accessed February 17, 2024. Available at: https://www.cms.gov/priorities/innovation/data-and-reports/2022/cmmi-strategy-refresh-imp-report

Claxton, G., Rae, M., Damico, A., Wager, E., Young, G., Whitmore, H. "Health Benefits in 2022: Premiums Remain Steady, Many Employers Report Limited Provider Networks for Behavioral Health". *Health Affairs* 2022 Oct. 27;41(11):1670–1680.

Health Affairs. "Value-Based Payment As A Tool To Address Excess US Health Spending". *Health Affairs Research Brief*, Published December 1, 2022. Last Accessed February 17, 2024. Available at: https://www.healthaffairs.org/do/10.1377/hpb20221014.526546/

Lewis, C., Horstman, C., Blumenthal, D., Abrams, M.K. "Value-Based Care: What It Is, and Why It's Needed". *Commonwealth Fund*, Feb. 7, 2023. https://www.commonwealthfund.org/publications/explainer/2023/feb/value-based-care-what-it-is-why-its-needed

Kaiser Family Foundation. "How Does U.S. Life Expectancy Compare to Other Countries". Published January 30, 2024. Last accessed February 17, 2024. Available at: https://www.healthsystemtracker.org/chart-collection/u-s-life-expectancy-compare-countries/#Life%20expectancy%20at%20birth,%20in%20years,%201980-2022

Koch, C., Roberts, K., Petruccelli, C., Morgan, D.J. "The Frequency of Unnecessary Testing in Hospitalized Patients". *American Journal of Medicine*. 2018;131(5):500–503.

National Opinion Research Center (NORC). "Evaluation of the Next Generation Accountable Care Organization (NGACO) Model". Final Report, Published January 2024. Last Accessed March 3, 2024. Available at: https://www.cms.gov/priorities/innovation/data-and-reports/2024/nextgenaco-sixthevalrpt

Shrank, W.H., Rogstad, T.L., Parekh, N. "Waste in the US Health Care System: Estimated Costs and Potential for Savings". *JAMA*. 2019;322(15):1501–1509.

Sinaiko, A.D., Landrum, M.B., Chernew, M.E. "Enrollment in a Health Plan with a Tiered Provider Network Decreased Medical Spending by 5 Percent". *Health Affairs*. 2017 May;36(5):870–875.

U.S. Government Accountability Office (GAO). "The Nation's Fiscal Health: Road Map Needed to Address Projected Unsustainable Debt Levels". Annual Report to Congress, February 2024.

Chapter 5

Healthcare Transformer 7: Health Equity

Identifying the causes of variation and disparity in care and, more importantly, identifying solutions to address these inequities are keystones of twenty-first-century medicine. The very definitions of the delivery of quality, safety, and value in healthcare are now increasingly aligned with that of care that is equitable, fair, and just. These challenge the traditional roles of healthcare delivery systems, which have long characterized health in terms of diagnoses, pills, and procedures. Counter to this, health is recognized as inextricably linked to variables that are social, financial, political, cultural, geographic, and racial. Successful healthcare organizations must not only acknowledge these but proactively commit to the delivery of care that seeks equity (Figure 5.1).

Healthcare Transformer 7 focuses on achieving better outcomes and lowering costs for all by implementing strategies to recognize and respond to inequities in health and healthcare delivery.

Problem

The U.S. healthcare system remains fragmented and challenged to provide access and treatment for even the most basic medical needs for certain populations.

DOI: 10.4324/9781003493914-5

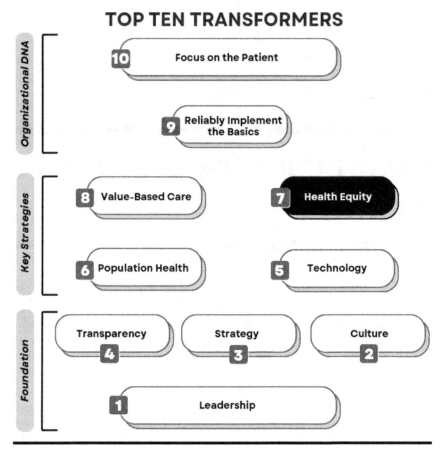

Figure 5.1 Top ten healthcare transformers.

As a result, sizable disparities in terms of care and outcomes remain pervasive. Consider these figures:

- 600,000: The number of Americans who experience homelessness on any given night. The number of sheltered adults older than age sixty-five in the US increased from 51,959 in 2020 to 61,121 in 2021. These numbers are expected to more than double by 2030. Housing insecurity is shown to raise the likelihood of untreated chronic health conditions, as well as the rate of emergency room presentation and hospitalization (Marill 2024).
- 20 years: The difference in life expectancy for an individual with an intellectual and developmental disability (IDD) compared with the average. When clinicians, clinical leaders, and executives at organizations were surveyed

on care for patients with IDD, 59% called current services insufficient, and only 15% indicated that their organization had accommodations for communication difficulties and complexity of care inherent to IDD (Gleason 2022).

■ The infant mortality rate for non-Hispanic Black babies is 2.4 times greater than that of non-Hispanic White babies (10.4 vs. 4.4) (CDC 2022).

■ Black patients who present to an emergency department, when compared with White counterparts with the same chief symptoms, have been shown to wait longer before being evaluated, receive a lower acuity score, have fewer imaging studies, and receive fewer pain medications (Joseph, Kennedy & Landry 2023).

By the end of 2023, 7.2% of all Americans lacked healthcare coverage. Such gaps in insurance lead to delayed or neglected care and inequitable access to health services. This number has improved from 16% in 2010 but remains at a level that suggests that substantial gaps exist for many Americans to have access to even basic health resources (White House 2024).

Though important, the problem extends beyond even the ability to access healthcare and extends into how healthcare is delivered and how it is received by each patient. Language, education, and disability among many other factors impact the capacity of patients to meaningfully connect with the healthcare system. To put this in terms of an all too common scenario, consider a patient with a third-grade educational level who is provided written or verbal health information at the eighth-grade level. How is that individual expected to read, comprehend, and follow along with the recommendations? Or what of the diabetic patient who lives in an inner-city apartment with no safe parks or grocery stores within a reachable distance? If they are instructed by their physician to seek healthy exercise and healthy eating, how are they to go about doing so? These are the sort of social and systemic barriers that create gaps in the ability of individuals to achieve health within their lives. They are also the exact sort of barriers that healthcare systems need to increasingly recognize and work with patients to overcome.

In 2019, the National Academies of Science, Engineering, and Medicine recommended that social risks be incorporated into healthcare on a routine basis. In addition, as of 2023, social risk screening has been included in the CMS Hospital Inpatient Quality Reporting System, the Joint Commission's accreditation programs, and the National Committee for Quality Assurance Healthcare Effectiveness Data and Information Set program (Fichtenberg & Fraze 2023). Yet despite this, as of 2022, nearly 1 out of 5 hospitals in the United States reported not collecting social needs data. Of those that do collect such data, only 54% noted doing so regularly. Among those areas that have the most disadvantaged patients, routine screening was found to be less frequent in lower-resourced hospitals compared to higher-resourced hospitals. Thus, not only is there inequity found in the health of patients, but also inequity apparent in the resources and infrastructure between healthcare organizations caring for these very patients (Chang 2023).

Transformer

In the last decade, there have been attempts by payors to address health equity within reimbursement models. Medicare has started to integrate measures of equity and diversity within its reports and has signaled that these will increasingly be measured within the definition of value and quality care delivery. Thus, payors are providing financial incentives to drive meaningful change and improvement. Defining the areas of inequity has been challenging because they are so ubiquitous. Models have emerged that characterize what has come to be called the social determinants of health (SDOH).

The Office of Disease Prevention and Health Promotion defines the SDOH as "The conditions in the environments where people are born, live, learn, work, play, worship, and age that affects a wide range of health, functioning, and quality-of-life outcomes". These include elements such as those within the HHS framework (Figure 5.2), which recognizes 5 fundamental social factors that influence health (HHS 2024).

These social factors, such as economic stability and neighborhood, can be further subdivided into more granular areas of impact. The healthcare literature continues to reveal that social determinants are more influential in shaping health outcomes than access to quality medical care (De Marchis, Alderwick & Gottlieb 2020). Thus, healthcare organizations must be prepared to engage in identification, through social risk screening, and response, through referral to nonmedical resources. This requires that adequate resources and services are available in the first place to meet these social needs.

A good place for any organization to start is to define the groups that are affected in the community that they serve. In particular, this requires shedding light upon the realities for those who disproportionately suffer from the poorest health outcomes. This must extend beyond demographics – and should include consideration of transportation, finances, social, cultural, linguistic, education, geography, and others. With the passage of the Affordable Care Act, all non-profit hospitals are mandated to complete a Community Health Needs Assessment (CHNA) every three years. The American Hospital Association provides a toolkit for hospitals and health systems to collaborate with their communities and strategic partners to both conduct an assessment and also to respond to areas of need (AHA 2023). The assessment includes the following steps:

Social Determinants of Health

Figure 5.2 Social determinants of health. **(Healthy People 2030, HHS Office of Disease Prevention and Health Promotion).**

1. Map development process
2. Build relationships
3. Develop community profile
4. Increase equity with data
5. Prioritize needs and assets
6. Document and communicate results
7. Plan equity strategy
8. Develop action plan
9. Evaluate progress

Traditional healthcare systems have generally operated passively, setting up services and then sitting back to wait for patients to walk through their doors. Initiatives to respond to the social determinants of health require more active and engaged approaches to create and foster connections. Pathways must be devised to proactively unite patients with resources, and this requires an understanding of the external environment. This includes an appreciation for the ecosystem in which SDOH programs operate, including those actors, factors, and relationships that influence capacity and results. Figure 5.3 details a pathway strategy that allows a stepwise approach to successful patient connection.

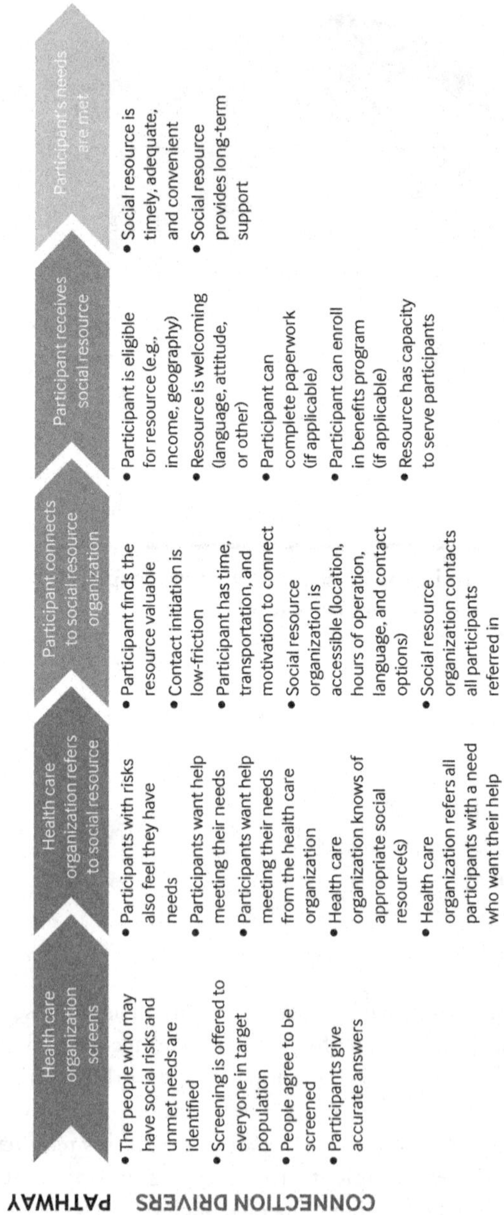

Figure 5.3 Social drivers of health pathway steps and connection Drivers (Schweitzer and Mohta, NEJM Catalyst, Massachusetts Medical Society, 2023, with permission).

Organizations should consider the following four processes as they evaluate and improve their pathways:

1. **Engage:** Engage stakeholders — including participants — in design and evaluation.
2. **Map:** Map the SDOH program goals, ecosystem, and pathway.
3. **Mitigate:** Mitigate potential failure points along the pathway.
4. **Measure and Improve:** Use process and qualitative analysis to improve pathway connection rates (Schweitzer & Mohta 2023).

Best Practices

Strategies for assessing social needs can often be tailored to specific demographics or issues faced among those of a given region, population, or disease. Organizations need to pay particular attention to cultural awareness and cultural competency.

Leadership in Equity and Diversity Council

Diversity and disparity are inextricably connected, and thus overcoming inequity requires inclusiveness. Seeking to ensure diversity of leadership and staff representative of the community, and to advance inclusion and eliminate healthcare disparities, Meritus Health has developed a Leadership in Equity and Diversity (LEAD) Council. The group brings together a representative cross-section of employees, providers, and management who desire to take action and affect positive change. The LEAD council performs training and education of employees and providers as well as fosters employee resource groups for several audiences, including the LGBTQ+ community. The goals of the LEAD council include:

- Ensuring that the diversity of leadership and staff is representative of the communities it serves
- Teaching leaders and staff how to understand and speak about cultural diversity-related topics such as color, race, age, gender identity, sexual orientation, ethnicity, or many other factors that make us all unique
- Raising general awareness and encouraging a culture of diversity, respect, and inclusion
- Creating ways to increase the inclusion of all people, with a specific focus on understanding unconscious bias and eliminating inequity and prejudice
- Learning and practicing intercultural competence and sensitive patient-centered care
- Building trusting & inclusive relationships within our community

LEAD Dashboard FY23									
Joy at Work	Metric	Calculation / Measure	FY2022 Baseline	Jul-22	Aug-22	Sep-22	Oct-22	FYTD	FY 2023 Target
Purpose	Employee Resource Groups	# of changes implemented presented by/feedback provided by ERG	NEW	0	1	2	0	3	10
Training	Lunch & Learn	# of Lunch and Learn sessions with 24/7 access	10	0	1	1	0	2	10
Training	Encourage a culture of diversity and respect	Strongly Agree & Agree Survey Results: Meritus Health cultivates a culture where people of all backgrounds are welcomed, heard and valued.	80%	n/a	n/a	n/a	n/a	80%	5% increase
Diversity	Rooney Rule	Implement policy	90.91%	1/1	1/2	2/2	Pending	80.00%	90%
Diversity	Overall Diversity	Total number of diverse employees (self disclosed) / total number of team members	15.92%	16.33%	17.62%	17.6%	Pending	17.57%	24.0%
Diversity	Diverse leadership workforce	Total number of diverse employees supervisor and above (self disclosed) / total number of team members supervisor and above	10.10%	11.17%	10.63%	10.2%	Pending	10.2%	24.0%
Diversity	Diverse nursing	Total number of diverse nursing team members (self disclosed) / total number of team members supervisor	10.10%	14.13%	15.28%	14.9%	Pending	14.9%	24.0%
Quality	Exclusively Breastfed	Difference in White versus Non-White Newborns Exclusively Breastfed	15.00%	7.8%	9.2%	7.6%	Pending	7.8%	3.5%
Quality	ED Opioid Administration	Difference in White versus Non-White Patient % receiving Opioids in the ED	5%	7.6%	8.0%	4.4%	6.0%	6.5%	3.5%
Quality	Poorly Controlled	Difference in White versus Non-White Patients % with Controlled Diabetes	7%	6.1%	5.3%	5.3%	Pending	5.6%	3.5%

Figure 5.4   Meritus health leadership in equity and disparity dashboard. Each measured metric is in alignment with organizational goals. Metrics are tracked and recorded monthly within the dashboard. The data presented runs from the beginning of fiscal year 2023 in July through October. (Meritus Health FY2022 Health Equity Report, Hagerstown, MD, 2022).

In practice, organizations must capture disparity measures in their "top quality" dashboard with a goal of zero disparity, similar to other patient safety measures. An example is ensuring all employees feel equally included in employee engagement and inclusion surveys. Figure 5.4 depicts the Meritus Health LEAD dashboard, a tracking tool for monitoring progress across key identified disparity measures.

Meritus Health also publishes an annual health equity report, summarizing the outcomes and progress of the health system's initiatives. Figure 5.5 depicts key findings from the 2022 report, including areas of priority and trended data for outcomes related to diabetes, sepsis, pre-term births, and c-sections. The data is used to set goals for improvement assigned to multidisciplinary action teams to help remediate disparities in care. For these best practices and programs, Meritus Health was awarded the 2023 Equity of Care Award by the American Hospital Association. As organizations advance their diversity initiatives they should:

1. Stratify their quality measures by race, ethnicity, language spoken, and other relevant important variables
2. Analyze the data to determine if disparities exist
3. Publish the report and share it widely
4. Start improvement projects

Figure 5.5 **Meritus health leadership in equity and disparity annual health equity report executive summary. (Meritus Health FY2022 Health Equity Report, Hagerstown, MD, 2022).**

Organizations must seek to identify disparities that lead to health inequities within the groups that they serve. This requires both a detailed understanding of the group as well as a connection to meaningful resources, or the development of new resources, within their communities.

Board Questions

As a health system board member, consider these questions:

1. Have we stratified our quality data by important demographic variables (race, ethnicity, language spoken, and others important to our population)?
2. What specific disparities in care do we have in our population?
3. Do we have teams with action plans working to reduce specific disparities in care?
4. How do the leadership and team members in our organization align with the demographics of the population we serve?
5. In what ways does our strategic plan address enhancing diversity, equity, and inclusion?
6. Does every member of our team, including leadership and frontline workers, go through unconscious bias training?

References

American Hospital Association. Community Health Assessment Toolkit. 2023. Last Accessed February 17, 2024. Available at: https://www.healthycommunities.org/resources/community-health-assessment-toolkit

Centers for Disease Control (CDC). "Infant Mortality in the United States, 2020: Data From the Period Linked Birth/Infant Death File". National Center for Health Statistics (U.S.) Published September 29 2022 Series: National Vital Statistics Reports, Volume 71, Number 5.

Chang, W., Richwine, C. "Social Needs Screening among Non-Federal Acute Care Hospitals, 2022". July 2023. ONC Data Brief, no. 67. Office of the National Coordinator for Health Information Technology: Washington DC.

Coughlin, S.S., Clary, C., Johnson, J.A., Berman, A., Heboyan, V., Benevides, T., Moore, J., George, V. "Continuing Challenges in Rural Health in the United States". *J Environ Health Sci.* 2019;5(2):90–92.

De Marchis EH, Alderwick H, Gottlieb LM. "Do Patients Want Help Addressing Social Risks?" *J Am Board Fam Med.* 2020;33:170–175.

Ely, D.M., Discoll, A.K. "Infant Mortality in the United States, 2018: Data from the Period Linked Birth/Infant Death File" National Vital Statistics Reports, vol. 69. No. 7. Hyattsville, MD: National Center for Health Statistics. 2020.

Fichtenberg, C., Fraze, T.K. "Two Questions Before Health Care Organizations Plunge into Addressing Social Risk Factors". *NEJM Catalyst.* 2023; 4(4). DOI: 10.1056/CAT.22.0400

Gleason, J. "Health Care Falls Short for Patients with Intellectual and Developmental Disabilities". *NEJM Catalyst.* 2022; 4(1). DOI: 10.1056/CAT.22.0441

Joseph JW, Kennedy M, Landry AM, et al. "Race and Ethnicity and Primary Language in Emergency Department Triage". *JAMA Netw Open.* 2023;6(10):e2337557.

Lee, R.J., Madan, R.A., Kim, J., Posadas, E.M., Yu, E.Y. "Disparities in Cancer Care and the Asian American Population". *The Oncologist.* 2021;26(6):453–460.

Marill, M.C. "For Some Patients, Better Health Starts with Finding a Home". *Health Affairs.* 2024; 43(2):150–155.

Meritus Health. "FY2022 Health Equity Report". Published June 2022. Last Accessed March 3, 2024. Available at: https://www2.meritushealth.com/files/Health-Equity-Report-FY22.FINAL-1.pdf

U.S. Department of Health and Human Services (HHS), Healthy People 2030, Office of Disease Prevention and Health Promotion. Last accessed February 13, 2024. Available at https://health.gov/healthypeople/objectives-and-data/social-determinants-health

Schweitzer, A., Mohta, N.S. "Pathways to Success in Meeting Health-Related Social Needs". *NEJM Catal.* 2023;4(4). DOI: 10.1056/CAT.22.0352

The White House. "Record Marketplace Coverage in 2024: A Banner Year for Coverage". Press Release Published January 24, 2024. Last Accessed February 17, 2024. Available at: https://www.whitehouse.gov/cea/written-materials/2024/01/24/record-marketplace-coverage-in-2024-a-banner-year-for-coverage/

Whitman, A., De Lew, N., Chappel, A., Aysola, V., Zuckerman, R., Sommers, B.D. "Addressing Social Determinants of Health: Examples of Successful Evidence-Based Strategies and Current Federal Efforts". Assistant Secretary for Planning and Evaluation, Office of Health Policy, April 1 2022 Report. Last Accessed February 17, 2024. Available at: https://aspe.hhs.gov/sites/default/files/documents/e2b650c d64cf84aae8ff0fae7474af82/SDOH-Evidence-Review.pdf

Chapter 6

Healthcare Transformer 6: Population Health

Healthcare delivery has traditionally emphasized the individual patient, and frequently the specific organ or disease within a patient. While such one-by-one patient care has value, as discussed previously in this text, taken as a whole it can be inefficient and even redundant. It also opens the possibility that something could be missed. Rather, organizations should seek the balance between care delivered in individualized episodes and care considered with a larger frame of reference. This is akin to stepping back and taking the 30,000-foot view of how to understand and best deliver care to bigger groups of individuals simultaneously. In recent decades there has been recognition that grouping patients with shared similarities, such as geography, illness, symptom, or other demographic, offers the opportunity to move beyond episodic medical care and to offer health and social services with larger-scaled interventions. In essence, this provides impact through higher quality, lower cost, and better care (Figure 6.1).

In this chapter, Healthcare Transformer 6 recognizes the ability to identify similar populations of patients and apply strategies to care for them at scale. These strategies are complementary to Transformer 7 and these build upon each other. Recognizing health inequities informs population health efforts to serve as responsive and even proactive action steps. This often involves engaging non-traditional entities within a community as well as public health agencies.

 DOI: 10.4324/9781003493914-6

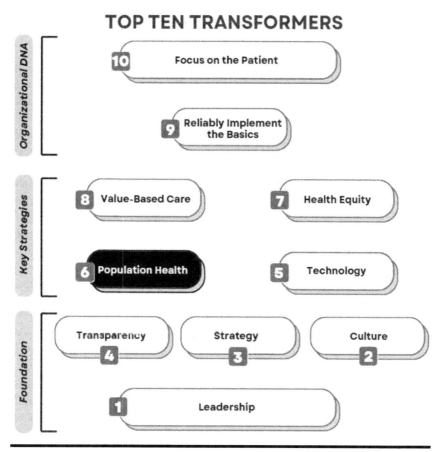

Figure 6.1   Top Ten healthcare transformers.

Problem

An estimated 6 out of every 10 adults in the US suffers from a chronic disease, such as hypertension, diabetes, heart disease, cancer, or others. Meanwhile, more than 40% live with multiple such chronic conditions (Carney et al. 2023). These diseases are responsible for almost $4 trillion in annual healthcare costs; and yet 5 of the 10 top leading causes of death in the US are, or are strongly associated with, preventable and treatable chronic diseases (Benavidez et al. 2024). Dividing care into each patient one by one, or worse each disease in each patient, is not only problematic and fragmented, but it can be profoundly inefficient and costly. Consider the following statistics:

- 46 million: The number of Americans, equal to around 15% of the total population, that live in a rural area. In these areas, there are on average 59.7 doctors per 100,000 people, compared to 125.3 per 100,000 in urban areas (Machado et al. 2021). As a result of this and other inequities, rural Americans are more likely to die from heart disease, cancer, unintentional injury, chronic lower respiratory disease, and stroke than their urban counterparts (CDC 2023).
- 66%: The percent of Medicare patients that have any visit with their primary care provider in a given year. That means that one out of three patients may be missing continuity and coordination of care. In the meanwhile, over 30% of patients see 5 or more different physicians per year. This risks the fragmenting of patient care and is worse for some populations of patients. Nationally, Black Medicare patients see doctors for one full less visit per year than White patients (7.24 visits per year vs. 8.23). (Barnett 2021).

The problem is complex and transcends the infrastructure of the healthcare system itself. So much so that it is predicted that only 20% of healthcare outcomes have anything to do with traditional clinical care, that is medications, procedures, tests, and counseling (Whitman et al. 2022). The other 80% relies upon an individual's day-to-day experiences, including their level of education, their access to healthy food, safe space for activity, and even access to healthcare. Where traditional healthcare has focused on clinical care, the reality is that health outcomes are far more predicated on healthy behaviors, the physical environment, and social and economic factors, as is depicted in Figure 6.2.

Meanwhile, medical education continues to train clinicians, including physicians, advanced practice providers, and nurses, in ways that encourage care silos. Ambulatory office schedules are filled to the brim with one-on-one in-person patient encounters, with little to no room in between or surrounding visits for population health management activities. Thus, the US health system is currently built around isolated and non-population-based care, with technologies, training, and infrastructure to reinforce these tendencies. Successful organizations are increasingly identifying opportunities to educate, redesign, and empower their teams to deliver care at a scale that provides population-level impacts.

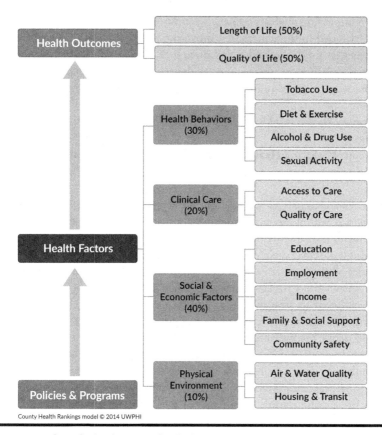

County Health Rankings model © 2014 UWPHI

Figure 6.2   The relative impact of policies, health factors, and health outcomes. (County Health Ratings, Wisconsin 2023).

Transformer

Populations can be identified as sharing a common geography or neighborhood, which contributes substantially to health in many ways. These include the number and quality of healthcare facilities, access to public transportation, as well as the presence of grocery stores, libraries, schools, safe spaces, and parks for recreation. Air quality and noise levels, for instance, can impact relative rates of asthma and sleep insufficiency (Arcaya, Ellen, & Steil 2024). Yet, despite sophisticated advancements in technologies that deliver care, such as surgical instruments and therapeutic medications; tools for assembling data on these varied social determinants of health (SDOH) remain comparatively rudimentary.

The Robert Wood Johnson Foundation (RFWJ) collects and publishes county-level data to build awareness of the factors that influence health and to support leaders in improving quality and health equity. Nearly every county in the United States is included in these measures, providing both context and comparison for conditions that influence health and outcomes. RFWJ publishes these rankings annually as well as a compendium of evidence-informed strategies that communities can use to respond to inequities and drive action. They can be accessed at:

- **County Health Rankings and Roadmaps:** https://www.countyhealthrankings.org
- **What Works for Health:** https://www.countyhealthrankings.org/strategies-and-solutions/what-works-for-health

In terms of characterizing a 'population', clusters of patients can either be grouped or subdivided within larger overarching populations. This could be as simple as identifying all the patients that an organization serves who have been diagnosed with a single disease, such as congestive heart failure. A step further would be to consider all those patients with this diagnosis who have been admitted to the hospital within the past 12 months. Additional demographics or variables can then be included to stratify similar populations, such as all Hispanic patients with congestive heart failure who live in a given zip code. The first major step, then, is to define the measures that matter and develop representative population groupings. This can be particularly important for marginalized, at-risk, or higher-cost populations. In many instances, these can be groups that may not access care in traditional ways or have other barriers to care. A population health approach allows a fuller appreciation for a panel of patients with similar characteristics. Once this population has been defined then connection, screening, management, and treatment options can be deployed at scale.

A 2020 CMS review identified 248 clinician-level measures applicable to population health and stratified these into six major areas (CMS 2021). The areas and some of these quality measures are denoted in Figure 6.3. This is not an exhaustive list, but rather a conceptual framework that has been put forward to identify areas of particular need and where gaps in services are significant. A good place to start would be to define a given population within an organization as noted above, taking into consideration variables such as similar disease states, demographics, or geographies. Then a review as to how this population compares to benchmarks and median numbers for any of the quality measures noted in Figure 6.3.

Population health represents this more sophisticated identification and analysis of patient groupings, with the goals of optimizing health outcomes, improving care, expanding access, and lowering costs. Taking a population health approach allows the clustering of large groups and tailoring initiatives to meet their shared needs.

Population Health Conceptual Framework

CMS Quality Measure Development Plan

Access to Care

Availability, Access to Behavioral Health, Foreign Language Interpretive Services, Health Insurance Coverage, Nutritional Support, Telehealth

Clinical Outcomes

Morbitidy Related to Opioids, Cancer, Premature Birth; Poor Birth Outcomes, Quality of Life, Recovery, Well-being

Coordination of Care and Community Services

Breastfeeding Support, Employment, Housing, Identification of Community Services, Integration of Mental Health, Pain Management, Referral to Community Services, Community Collaboration, Social Support, Transitions in Care

Health Behaviors

Health Literacy, Nutrition/Malnutrition, Obesity, Physical Activity, Safe Medication Disposal, Smoking, Accident Prevention for Head or Seat Belt Injury, Distracted Driving

Preventive Care and Screening

Abuse and Neglect, Cancer Screening for Protaste, Caregiver Risk Assessment, Comprehensive Substance Use Disorder Screening, Family Planning for Interconception Care, Medication Reconciliation, Psychosocial Needs, Screening for Alcohol or Tobacco Abuse

Utilization of Health Services

Emergency Department Use

Figure 6.3 CMS population health conceptual framework. (CMS Quality Measures Development Plan, Bethesda, MD, 2021).

Best Practices

Building upon a recognition of inherent health inequities, there are countless opportunities for population health to transform healthcare. Some case studies that demonstrate emerging best practices that change lives and care delivery for specific populations:

Housing for Health

As recognized in Chapter 5, populations that experience homelessness have substantially worse health outcomes and result in a disproportionately higher cost to health systems. As a result, many healthcare organizations have started to invest in programs that support community space and affordable housing. One 2020 study showed that from 2017–2019, 52 hospitals and health systems across the US committed $1.6 billion in such housing-related investments (Garcia et al. 2024).

One example is the 'Housing for Health' initiative in Baltimore, Maryland at Bon Secours Hospital, a community hospital with 72 licensed beds and annual operating revenues of approximately $121 million. The organization has a community with a high concentration of poverty, African American residents, and vacant homes. The system has purchased, repurposed, and developed 801 units as affordable housing across 12 properties. These serve low-income individuals, families, people with disabilities, and seniors. Each includes a service coordinator supporting and connecting residents to services. The properties also have wireless internet, a computer lab, a gym, social events, and produce box delivery. The program has found that for every 1 dollar spent they generate an annual $1.30 net social and $1.92 economic return. They have also recognized the impact of improved health, lower costs, and increased access and connections for this population (Drabo et al. 2021).

Community Health Navigators

Responding to the social determinants of health and social needs requires new team members and techniques, outside those traditional models and infrastructure of healthcare delivery. AmeriHealth Caritas implemented a Community Health Navigator program to address a targeted high and emerging-risk population of its Medicaid members. This population was screened specifically for SDOH, and gaps were addressed with tailored interventions. The team included navigators as well as community care managers who delivered services directly to member homes. The program realized a 9.7% decrease in emergency department visits, a 30% reduction in inpatient admissions, and an 11% reduction in healthcare spending (Pfeiffer et al. 2022).

Care Callers

Within the first year of screening patients for social determinants of health, Meritus Health identified over 1,000 patients who acknowledged a lack of companionship. Their data showed that one in twelve patients reported experiencing loneliness in the prior week. Loneliness and social isolation have been shown to impact life expectancy as much as smoking, obesity, and physical inactivity. This population has a 50% higher risk of dementia, a 29% increased risk of heart disease, and a 32% higher risk of stroke (NASEM 2020). As a response, Meritus developed the Care Callers program, matching volunteer callers to check in on patients' well-being, offer conversation and connection, and provide links to resources, including food, transportation, and grief counseling. The program set a goal of 50% of enrollees reporting they are less lonely within 4 months of engagement with program intervention. Calls to patients 1–2 times per week for 10–15 minutes aimed to support adults with reducing isolation, coping, and depression. In the two years since the program was started, more than 70 volunteer Care Callers and two paid care callers have called over 500 people and call 300 people on a routine basis. One of the lonely residents has since become a Care Caller. Individuals in the program are asked 4 months after being called if they are less lonely and 95% say they are less lonely from the one question survey.

Care to Share

Food insecurity impacts those with limited or uncertain access to adequate food and is associated with increased risk for cardiovascular disease, obesity, type 2 diabetes, hypertension, birth defects, cognitive problems, and mental illness. It is estimated that healthcare expenditures related to food insecurity reach $53 billion annually (Bleich et al. 2023). In Washington County, Maryland, 13% of people are considered food insecure, and 15% of children also fall into that category. While screening patients for food insecurity may provide the opportunity to connect them to community resources or assistance programs, there is often a few days delay before patients have access to the benefits. This could mean a few days without food. To overcome this barrier, Meritus Health initiated the Care to Share program, placing food donation units at three high-traffic areas in their health system, outside the main hospital entrance, the emergency department, and a primary care clinic. The concept is simple, using old pyxis medication dispensing machines, anyone is encouraged to "take what you need and give if you can", similar to the little free library concept. The units are also refilled by the health system, with an investment of nearly $100,000 per year.

Each of these are examples of programs that identified a target and at-risk population and then integrated social care into healthcare delivery in pursuit of improved health, well-being, and equity for that population.

Board Questions

As a health system board member, consider these questions:

1. How does our organization develop and implement population health initiatives?
2. For which patient populations can we be providing better value?
3. What is an example of a health inequity that we sought to improve with a population health approach?
4. Which non-medical care factors that impact health status are we addressing the most and what factor is next?
5. Which social determinants of health are we impacting the most?
6. How do we prioritize different population health initiatives in our organization?

References

Arcaya, M., Ellen, I.G., Steil, J. "Neighborhoods and Health: Interventions at the Neighborhood Level Could Help Advance Health Equity". *Health Affairs.* 2024;43(2):156–163.

Barnett, M.L., Bitton, A., Souza, J., Landon, B.E. "Trends in Outpatient Care for Medicare Beneficiaries and Implications for Primary Care, 2000-19". *Ann Intern Med* 2021;174(12):1658–1665.

Benavidez, G.A., Zahnd, W.E., Hung, P., Eberth, J.M. "Chronic Disease Prevalence in the US: Sociodemographic and Geographic Variations by Zip Code Tabulation Area". *Prev Chronic Dis* 2024;21:230267.

Bleich, S.N., Koma, J.W., Jernigan, V.B.B. The Worsening Problem of Food Insecurity. *JAMA Health Forum.* 2023;4(11):e234974.

Carney, T.J., Wiltz, J.L., Davis, K., Briss, P.A., Hacker, K. "Advancing Chronic Disease Practice Through the CDC Data Modernization Initiative". *Prev Chronic Dis* 2023;20:230120.

Centers for Disease Control and Prevention (CDC). "About Rural Health". Published November 28, 2023. Last Accessed February 21, 2024. Available at: https://www.cdc.gov/ruralhealth/about.html

Centers for Medicare & Medicaid Services, Health Services Advisory Group. CMS Quality Measure Development Plan 2020 Population Health Environmental Scan and Gap Analysis Report for the Quality Payment Program. Baltimore, MD: Centers for Medicare & Medicaid Services; 2021. Last Accessed February 21, 2024. Available at: https://www.cms.gov/Medicare/Quality-Payment-Program/Measure-Development/Measure-development

Drabo, E.F., Eckel, G., Ross, S.L., Brozic, M., Carlton, C.G., Warren, T.Y., et al. "A Social-Return-On-Investment Analysis of Bon Secours Hospital's 'Housing for Health' Affordable Housing Program". *Health Affairs.* 2021;40(3):513–520.

Garcia, C., Doran, K., Kushel, M. "Homelessness and Health: Factors, Evidence, Innovations That Work, And Policy Recommendations". *Health Affairs.* 2024;43(2):164–171.

Machado, S.R., Jayawardana, S., Mossialos, E., Vaduganathan, M. Physician Density by Specialty Type in Urban and Rural Counties in the US, 2010 to 2017. *JAMA Netw Open.* 2021;4(1):e2033994.

National Academies of Sciences, Engineering, and Medicine. (NASEM). *Social Isolation and Loneliness in Older Adults: Opportunities for the Health Care System.* 2020. Washington, DC: The National Academies Press.

Pfeiffer, E.J., DePaula, C.L., Flores, W.O., Lavallee, A.J. "Barriers to Patients' Acceptance of Social Care Interventions in Clinic Settings". *American Journal of Preventive Medicine.* 2022;63(3)S116–S121.

The University of Wisconsin Population Health Institute. "County Health Rankings & Roadmaps", 2023. Last Accessed March 7, 2024. Available at: www.countyhealthrankings.org

Whitman, A., De Lew, N., Chappel, A., Aysola, V., Zuckerman, R., Sommers, B.D. "Addressing Social Determinants of Health: Examples of Successful Evidence-Based Strategies and Current Federal Efforts". Assistant Secretary for Planning and Evaluation, Office of Health Policy, April 1 2022 Report. Last Accessed February 17, 2024. Available at: https://aspe.hhs.gov/sites/default/files/documents/e2b650c d64cf84aae8ff0fae7474af82/SDOH-Evidence-Review.pdf

Chapter 7

Healthcare Transformer 5: Technology

Advancement of technology has served as the foundation of disruptive innovations across essentially every industry and has inspired emerging markets, customers, revenue sources, and businesses. US healthcare is no different, though uptake and integration of technology have tended to progress slightly slower in its spread in this industry.

The promise of the impact of technology on better health and healthcare is profound. On one hand, health and outcomes can be vastly improved through the successful application of electronic health records (EHRs), remote digital monitoring, artificial intelligence (AI), and many others. At the same time, these technologies have the potential to revolutionize healthcare delivery and the very frameworks in which patients seek and access care.

Healthcare Transformer 5 (Figure 7.1) focuses on the optimal implementation of technology to achieve better healthcare outcomes and make our health system more efficient.

Problem

In recent years, goals for meaningfully connecting with patients to improve their health have expanded beyond the typical walls of hospitals and clinics. New technologies have allowed patients to receive care in innovative ways from a variety of healthcare team members, including digital platforms and remote tracking of

DOI: 10.4324/9781003493914-7

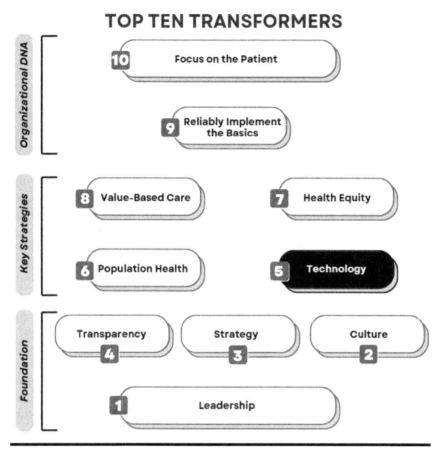

Figure 7.1 Top ten healthcare transformers.

measures of health. Meanwhile, the use of paper, manual processes, and the lack of clinical decision support systems continue and these are key reasons for medical errors and patient and provider dissatisfaction. Medication errors are very common, as shown by the following estimates:

■ Medication errors cause at least one death every day and injure approximately 1.3 million people annually in the United States (WHO 2017).
■ 10% of patients admitted to the hospital will have an adverse event or harm, with medication errors and adverse drug events the most common cause. Of these 1 out of every 3 are preventable (Bates et al. 2023).

There is a multitude of reasons that medication errors occur, including giving the wrong dose, the wrong drug, the wrong administration of the drug, a drug-drug interaction, or a drug-allergy interaction. Technology is one important approach to improving these outcomes through better connectedness and communication between systems, alert monitoring, automation, and point-of-care decision support tools.

There have been massive improvements in technological integration over the past two decades, in particular the adoption of EHRs. In 2009 just 6.6% of health systems across the US had even basic electronic records, and this had skyrocketed to 96% of all hospitals by the end of 2021 (Office of the National Coordinator, 2022 & Jiang et al. 2023). Despite this our healthcare system remains filled with paper, faxing of documents is far too common, and healthcare providers are among the only professionals left still frequently utilizing pagers. These cause great inefficiency in time and resources and have led to a tremendous level of delays in communication, as well as miscommunication, medical errors, and worse healthcare. Paper and manual systems mean more dependence on human processes and memory, which are less reliable and lead to more mistakes.

Much of the growth in EHR adoption can be credited to the Health Information Technology for Economic and Clinical Health (HITECH) Act of 2009. In this, Congress set aside $27 billion for an incentive program that encouraged hospitals and providers to adopt electronic health records systems (Sood, Bates, and Sheikh, 2015). Despite near universal implementation, EHR systems are still not yet ideal today. While many platforms were developed, few were built to communicate with each other, and scant standards for interoperability have been established. This means that hospitals and clinics do not always have the ability to share information digitally. For patients traveling on vacation, or those seeing multiple outpatient specialists, this often means different patient medical records, histories, or testing results all stored in separate silos with different health systems or offices. One study showed that only 45% of hospitals maintained fully interoperable health record systems that could send and receive data to other sites. This same study suggests that universal interoperability is not likely to occur before 2027 (Holmgren, Everson, and Adler-Milstein 2022). Thus, it is projected to be a full 18 years from the passage of the HITECH Act until hospitals have meaningful digital records that share patient information. This highlights the major problem with integrating technology into the US healthcare system.

Transformer

The meaningful implementation of technology has a major, positive impact on all key players in the healthcare system. Although there is no perfect system, and even the best is constantly evolving and innovating, the presence of a system can support how healthcare teams deliver better care and help patients and families be more involved in the management of their care.

The recent development of EHRs has allowed the electronic conversion of the paper medical chart into a digital medium. EHRs include a patient's medical history, test results, current medicines, treatment plans, and information that can help the clinician manage the patient's health. In a simple analogy, EHRs may be compared to computer accounting systems. These have expanded rapidly and increasingly provide bidirectional communication options for patients, alongside digital transmission of test results and medical documents. These efforts empower patients, providing ease of access, reminder systems, and detailed information about their health, medications, and treatment plans. In addition to changing the context in which patient information is transmitted, these technologies are shifting where and how patients interface with healthcare systems. While the COVID-19 pandemic accelerated telemedicine adoption, there were indications throughout the prior decade that the industry was moving in the direction of more virtual care. Studies in 2022 showed that more than 4 in 10 patients (43%) used telehealth during that year and upwards of two-thirds of patients in rural areas were actively using digital patient portals (Chang et al. 2024 & Pullyblank et al. 2023).

In recent years, a rapidly growing area of technology in healthcare has been artificial intelligence and machine learning. AI and machine learning process historical and real-time data through algorithms that seek to predict outcomes or recommend treatment options. These technologies stand to transform how care is delivered and how it is experienced. For clinical team members, this means the rapid review of thousands of pages of historical patient information instantaneously, voice recognition software to dictate and document care encounters, or point-of-care clinical decision support. For patients, this may mean instant virtual access to a clinician, predictive tools or guidance for a constellation of symptoms, real-time text messaging with the healthcare team, and unfettered access and portability for their healthcare records. Thus, generative AI has the potential to greatly improve and even transform healthcare.

The technology transformer requires a hospital to:

- Conduct an assessment to identify the gaps for implementation
- Develop a detailed roadmap
- Learn from other sites that have experience and expertise in implementation
- Identify champions and areas with which to start
- Provide ongoing education and support

- Go beyond technology and pay attention to change management, work-flow redesign, human resource implications, and leadership drive
- Stay focused on implementation

If not well planned and implemented, such systems may not achieve their full benefits. However, healthcare must embrace technology to further health outcomes. Technology will continue to develop rapidly, and hospitals must continue to work on the effective and efficient implementation of technology to achieve their maximum potential.

Best Practices

There are numerous areas in which technology is impacting healthcare delivery with improved cost and quality. Some case studies that demonstrate emerging best practices that transform patient care:

Data Visualization and Analysis

Technology platforms allow the rapid collection of a multitude of data that can be visualized and analyzed to evaluate processes and outcomes as well as to trend performance. Meritus Health has developed such a technological platform with its Data Atlas program, which tracks metrics across the health system. This includes care areas from the operating room and intensive care unit, to their home health agency, primary care, and many more. Figure 7.2 depicts a sample data visualization screen used to track emergency department throughput measures. Real-time and historical data are used to compare daily, monthly, and annual metrics. This can be segmented in many ways to break down care delivery, such as the time from a patient's arrival to their initial triage or the time spent getting a CT scan.

Clinical Decision Support Tools

Technology integrated within electronic medical record platforms allows real-time recommendations and point-of-care clinical decision support. This includes information for best practices, diagnosis, testing, and treatment. These can be integrated as passive recommendations or mandatory interventions and provide immediate data as well as the ability to hardwire processes. A case study of clostridium difficile infection (CDI) rates at Meritus Health, which were nearly double the national expected value, demonstrates the impact of these tools.

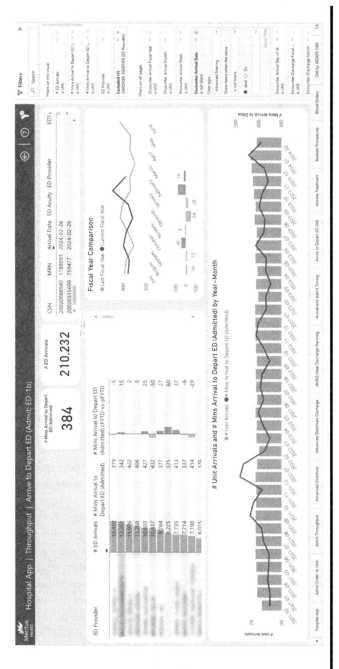

Figure 7.2 **Emergency department data display and metrics. The bottom graph depicts the average minutes from patient arrival to departure trended by month. The top right displays this information in comparison to the previous fiscal year. The top left shows discharge time by physician assigned to the patient.**

Source: Data Atlas at Meritus Health, Hagerstown, MD.

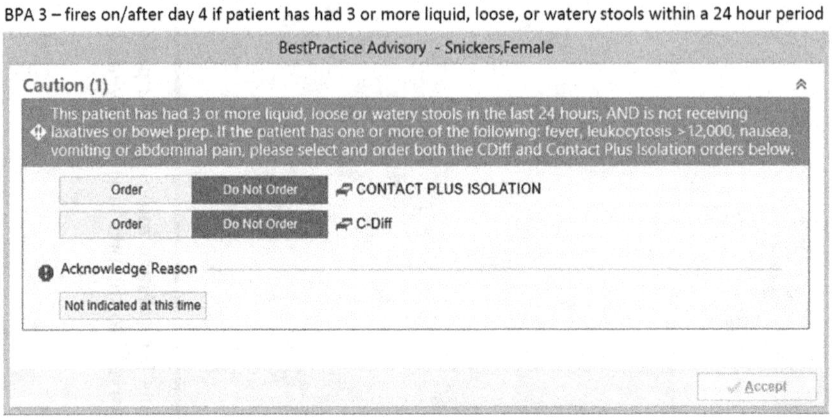

BPA 3 – fires on/after day 4 if patient has had 3 or more liquid, loose, or watery stools within a 24 hour period

Figure 7.3 Clinical decision support best practice advisory. Clostridium Difficile testing BPA prompt that is depicted at the point of care in the electronic medical record.

Source: EPIC electronic medical record at Meritus Health, Hagerstown, MD.

At the outset of the improvement initiative, CDI was found to be overdiagnosed in the hospital. Of those testing positive, 21% did not demonstrate typical symptoms of diarrhea, 71% were on stool softeners or laxatives, and 77% were determined to not need treatment due to colonization prior to hospitalization. Each of these are among best practices to limit testing and treatment. Meritus deployed a nursing best practice advisory (BPA) in the electronic medical record to inform the nurse if ordering a test after the third day of hospitalization. Figure 7.3 depicts this BPA for C.diff testing. clinical decision support tool algorithms can be designed intentionally, and Figure 7.4 depicts the logic that the improvement team devised to trigger the BPA.

Initially, nurses overrode or bypassed this BPA 29% of the time. Following, the nursing BPA was modified to prevent the nurse from ordering C.diff testing after hospital day three with a hard stop. This forcing function then required the attending provider to evaluate the patient, which subsequently resulted in providers continuing to override the BPA. Again, the BPA was modified with additional clinical logic that included requirement of an infectious disease chart review to approve the patient presentation. Such Implementation of this hard stop at the point of ordering CDI rates were significantly decreased CDI rates, as depicted in Figure 7.5, and have sustained improvement through multiple years exceeding the target.

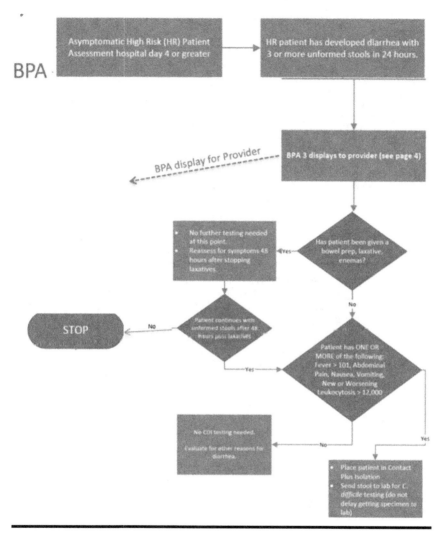

Figure 7.4 Algorithm for clostridium difficile inpatient clinical decision support best practice advisory.

Source: Meritus Health, Hagerstown, MD.

Electronic Patient Portal

Technology allows patients to review their complete healthcare records, and increasingly to have ownership over them. Meritus Health utilizes the EPIC MyChart platform for patients to access and interact with their health as well as

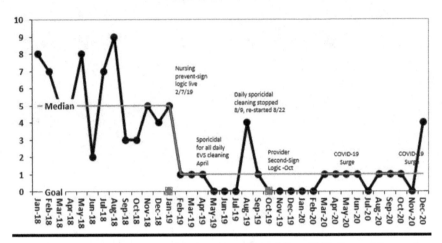

Figure 7.5 Run chart for monthly inpatient clostridium difficile positive testing at Meritus Health. The chart depicts the rate of positive testing from January 2018 through December 2020, with months on the X axis and number of positive tests on the Y axis. Significant decreases are observed following implementation of nursing BPA in February 2019 and provider BPA in September 2019.

Source: Meritus Health, Hagerstown, MD.

connect with their healthcare team. Figure 7.6 depicts a sample patient's digital MyChart home screen, which patients can access from their mobile device or computer. The left-hand menu offers patients the ability to schedule appointments, including real-time urgent or virtual visits, as well as to message their care team directly, review test results, or reorder medications. Patients can update their medical history, and what matters most for their care, and engage in targeted education modules tailored for them.

Artificial Intelligence Predictive Analytics Tools

Technologies allow continuous monitoring and analysis of large and developing data sets. While a nurse may assess a patient's blood pressure a few times each day, or a physician review laboratory results for a few moments each morning, machine learning can continuously review and assess patient measures of health or illness. This can be used for detection as well as predictive modelling. One example is the risk stratification and early prediction for a patient progressing to sepsis. Sepsis, a potentially severe complication of infection in the body, is associated with significant morbidity and mortality. Nationally, there are

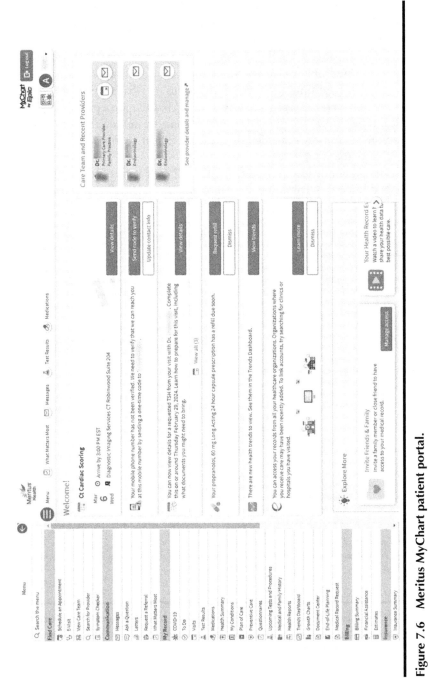

Figure 7.6 Meritus MyChart patient portal.

Source: EPIC System used by Meritus Health, Hagerstown, MD.

approximately 270,00 deaths per year and a cost of $38 billion related to sepsis in the US (Hollenbeak et al. 2023). Emerging models are integrated within electronic medical records, continuously screening the patient based on data collection (vital signs, labs etc.) and updating every 15 min to assess for changes in condition that could indicate sepsis. Monitoring clinical changes in a patient's condition provides real-time alerts with instructions on what steps to take next. Figure 7.7 depicts a critical sepsis advisory warning, based upon a predictive algorithm. Real-time clinical care decisions and ordering are immediately prompted to the healthcare team. Meanwhile, the patient's digital chart will also change color to indicate the rising risk.

What should not be lost in these examples and their results is the significant planning and leadership commitment it took to put these technology solutions

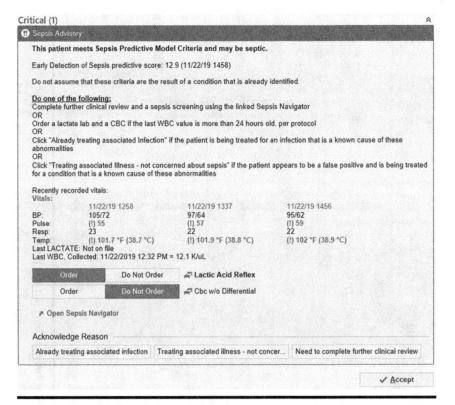

Figure 7.7 Sepsis predictive model advisory. The screen depicts a predictive scoring based upon specific criteria as well as real-time recommendations for next steps for ordering and patient care.

Source: EPIC System used by Meritus Health, Hagerstown, MD.

in place and achieve the results in improved productivity, reduced costs, and improved quality. Without the purposeful design, patience, and backing from leadership and governance, these results would have been much more difficult and time-consuming to accomplish.

Board Questions

As a health system board member, consider these questions:

1. What is our technology strategy and operating plan?
2. Are we on track with the implementation of our various technology systems?
3. Approximately what percentage of our workflow is not paperless?
4. Are there other innovative or disruptive organizations in our marketplace or community that are using technologies that we do not?
5. How do patients access their medical records and connect with their healthcare team, and are there opportunities to improve?
6. How is, or will, our organization apply artificial intelligence to deliver care?

References

Bates, D., Levine, D., Salmasian, H., Syrowatka, A., Shahian, D., Lipsitz, S., et al. "The Safety of Inpatient Health Care", *New England Journal of Medicine*, 2023;388:142–153.

Hollenbeak, C.S., Henning, D.J., Geeting, G.K., Ledeboer, N.A., Farugi, I.A., Pierce, C.G., et al. "Costs and Consequences of a Novel Emergency Department Sepsis Diagnostic Test: The IntelliSep Index". *Critical Care Explorations*. 2023;5(7):e0942.

Holmgren, A.J., Everson, J., Adler-Milstein, J. "Association of Hospital Interoperable Data Sharing with Alternative Payment Model Participation". *JAMA Health Forum*. 2022;3(2):e215199.

Jiang, J., Qi, K., Bai, G., Shulman, K. "Pre-Pandemic Assessment: A Decade of Progress in Electronic Health Record Adoption Among U.S. Hospitals". *Health Affairs Scholar*, 2023;1(3).

Office of the National Coordinator for Health Information Technology. Adoption of Electronic Health Records by Hospital Service Type 2019–2021, *Health IT Quick Stat #60*. April 2022.

Pullyblank, K., Krupa, N., Scribani, M., Chapman, A., Kern, M., Brunner, W. "Trends in Telehealth Use Among a Cohort of Rural Patients During the COVID-19 Pandemic". *Digit Health* 2023;3(9):20552076231203803.

Sood, H. S., Bates, D. W., Sheikh, A. "Leveraging Health Information Technology to Achieve the Triple Aim," *The Commonwealth Fund Blog*, Jan. 5, 2015.

World Health Organization "WHO Launches Global Effort to Halve Medication-Related Errors in 5 Years. News Release, March 29, 2017. Last Accessed January 24, 2024. Available at: https://www.who.int/news/item/29-03-2017-who-launches-global-effort-to-halve-medication-related-errors-in-5-years

Chang, E., Penfold, R.B., Berkman, N.D. "Patient Characteristics and Telemedicine Use in the US, 2022". *JAMA Netw Open.* 2024;7(3):e243352. https://jamanetwork.com/journals/jamanetworkopen/fullarticle/2816685

Chapter 8

Healthcare Transformer 4: Transparency

There are continuous calls for public awareness and mandatory reporting of quality information by hospitals and health systems. How is your organization responding?

Transparency is a transformative factor in our healthcare system (see Figure 8.1). This chapter will provide examples of public reporting that have spurred organizations to quality improvement efforts and examine how consumers are increasingly using data for decision-making and discussion with their providers and healthcare teams.

The leadership message from this transformer is to embrace transparency as a change agent—whether it is to provide public reporting of the organization's quality outcomes, employee and patient satisfaction survey results, ethics policies, financial assistance policies, or conflicts of interest.

Problem

Without transparency, it is difficult to make informed decisions. For example, one only needs to look at the 2000s housing crisis to see the risks associated with inadequate public reporting of financial information. Buyers of mortgage-backed securities and collateralized debt obligations did not fully realize the risky nature

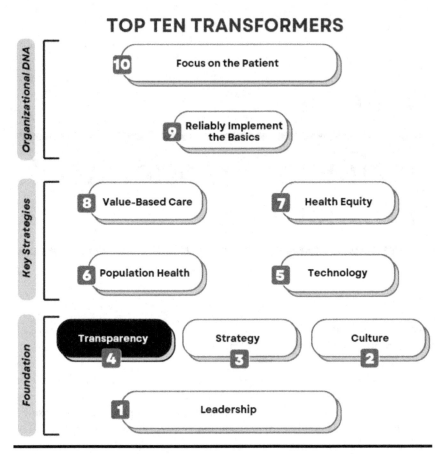

Figure 8.1 Top ten healthcare transformers.

of their investments. Trust was placed in the high credit ratings such investments received because sufficient information was not available about the nature of the individual assets and how the credit ratings were assigned (Kroszner 2008). Greater transparency is needed to "give all parties better tools to monitor financial risk-taking themselves" (Baily and Litan 2008).

Without readily accessible quality information, consumers are similarly hampered in their healthcare choices. For instance, 60% of patients report that they want more information than they currently have when they are deciding where to get care (Cordina & Greenberg 2020); 90% want to know the costs of care before care delivery (Energy and Commerce 2023). When surveyed nearly 1 in 4 patients believe that proof or evidence of outcomes and good results is the most important factor in their confidence that they would receive high-quality care from an organization (Cordina & Greenberg 2020). The release of performance data has been proposed to impact quality in multiple ways. The first is through selection, in which consumers choose better performers and thus motivate organizations to improve to become more attractive. Meanwhile, the identification of quality deficits may also stimulate the organizational or individual desire to seek improvement (Berwick et al. 2003). Although consumer use of healthcare quality information is still growing, there is evidence that public reporting has increased quality and outcomes. These include small improvements in mortality, such as for cardiac surgery (Campanella et al. 2016).

A shift is occurring as increasingly empowered patients are now considered consumers of healthcare, with more choice and autonomy than ever before. These are the same individuals who have become accustomed to making purchasing or dining decisions based upon online posted reviews on Amazon or Yelp, as well as sought transportation options with Uber. Similarly, one survey found that up to 90% of patients use online reviews as part of their evaluation of physicians, and almost 3 out of 4 (71%) use online reviews as a first step to finding a new doctor (Morris 2020). Put simply, organizations that share more information and cultivate an online presence will more meaningfully connect with their patients.

Rising healthcare costs extend well beyond the systemic level, and can lead to drastic financial burdens for patients and families. Roughly one out of every five Americans have debt related to medical care, and a staggering 62% of bankruptcies are related to medical debt (Commonwealth Fund 2023). This means that transparency and expectations for the pricing of medical care influence decision-making for patients, and will increasingly drive competition between organizations. As of 2021, federal law has required hospitals to publicly post information about their standard prices and negotiate discount rates for common health services to encourage consumers to compare prices and to promote competition. However, since the passage of the law, actual compliance has been inconsistent and has created confusion for patients. There remains a lack of specificity and standardization in what hospitals must report and how they report it (Kaiser 2023). However, savvy organizations are finding ways to communicate competitive financial advantages to their patients.

Transformer

As a hospital board member, you can use public reporting as a tool to assess the organization's performance and areas for improvement. Leaders often worry about public perception of hospital performance once data are publicly reported. However, do not let perfect be the enemy of very good. Be transparent with your data internally and externally. Use your hospital website to share quality information, employee and patient satisfaction survey data, ethics policies, and conflicts of interest. Going a step further, this information should be posted visibly in public areas throughout the system, such as in lobbies and common hallways. Clearly communicate that your hospital is dedicated to improving the community's health, and to do so, you must enhance your systems.

It may be helpful to think of the transformative opportunity to increase transparency in terms of the following model, which incorporates four key factors:

1. Establish clear transparency values: Develop sound transparency principles to guide decisions. Essential questions to ask include:
   ■ What organizations are we comparing ourselves to?
   ■ What are our goals?
   ■ What measures do we use?
   ■ What information do we share?
   ■ Are we reporting positive and negative data?
2. Draw meaningful comparisons: Set appropriate goals to ensure significant comparisons.
   ■ Compare your performance over time to track progress.
   ■ Compare your performance to others—not just the state or national average, but a benchmark. For example, compare short- and long-term goals with the best in your health system, the best in the state, the best in the nation, and the best among your peers. Avoid complacency with your comparisons. Remember that benchmarks can serve as a floor or a ceiling.
3. Create accountability for results: Build accountability by reviewing measures and linking them to financial performance. Translate data into lives saved, complications avoided, and dollars saved. Use metrics that make the gaps more understandable and meaningful in terms of individuals affected. For example, 90% might seem good, but not when 10% could mean an infection a day. Tie increased transparency to employee incentives as appropriate.
4. Acknowledge the journey: Much progress is yet to come in the area of transparency. We need to improve in measuring and using data, publicizing the availability of quality data, and helping consumers understand the information.

It is not only essential to consider all aspects of transparency and to share your information but also to empower patients to understand it. This means more than just posting quality metrics on your website or a bulletin board. Rather, this means helping your patients and your community to understand what they mean and what you are doing about them. Figure 8.2 depicts the elements of how a well-informed consumer can lead to higher value in healthcare.

How Well-Informed Consumer Choices Can Lead to Higher-Value Health Care

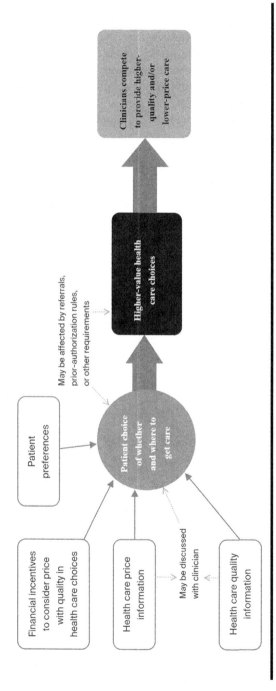

Figure 8.2 How well-informed consumer choices can lead to higher-value healthcare.

Source: Sinaiko, A., Bambury, E., and Chien, A. "Consumer Choice in U.S. Health Care: Using Insights from the Past to Inform the Way Forward". Commonwealth Fund, November 2021.

Best Practices

Along with reporting of quality measures, costs, and outcomes, it is important for organizations to publicly share information about their efforts. This may include success stories from amazing patient experiences or new service line developments or offerings. However, organizations should also seek to be transparent about needed areas of improvement, and even at times, failures. The key is that these are shared in a transparent way that can promote trust, integrity, and the desire for continuous improvement.

Publishing Diversity and Health Disparity Data

Meritus Health is transparent about its organizational and community efforts in diversity and health equity. On its website (https://www.meritushealth.com/about/diversity-and-health-equity), Meritus transparently publishes its internal diversity data as well as details on health disparities that are recognized in quality outcomes. Meritus shares this data proactively with the local newspaper and other public and community entities. The message is that disparities do exist in the community and population served, and efforts are ongoing to eliminate those disparities. The health system transparently shares these for publication in local newspapers for public and community awareness. There have been no negative consequences from the public reporting and the action and transparency have increased engagement on this issue.

Patient Satisfaction Data

As another approach to transparency, a number of health systems share their patient satisfaction data by physician. Duke Health is an example of one health system that displays on their website, in their find a doctor section, the overall patient satisfaction score by provider. Figure 8.3 is an example that compares three of their primary care doctors. By providing this information, individuals can see the numerical patient satisfaction scores and written comments. It is another piece of information that people can use in selecting a provider. There may be perceived bias that an organization is sharing their own data, however, many people feel a greater sense of trust that information is being shared at all.

Figure 8.3   Duke health provider webpage comparison example.

Source: https://www.dukehealth.org/find-doctors-physicians/compare?back =m%253D0%2526m1%253DSpecialist%2526m2%253DPrimary%252520Care %2526sc%253D60%2526c%253D1052741__483583__987869&id=1052741& id=483583&id=987869 Accessed 3/31/24.

Board Questions

As a hospital board member, consider these questions:

1. How does our organization compare on publicly reported indicators?
2. Are we publishing our own data on our website? Why or why not?
3. Are we educating staff well enough on these measures and our philosophy?
4. Are we educating the community on these publicly reported quality measures?
5. Are we transparent not just on data, but on key practices and policies, such as how we collect patient payments or how we communicate medical errors?
6. Do we transparently share our prices in a way that is clear and easy to understand?

References

Baily, M.N., Litan, R.E. "A Brief Guide to Fixing Finance. Washington, DC: The Brookings Institution". Published September 2008. Last Accessed February 27, 2024. Available at: https://www.brookings.edu/wp-content/uploads/2016/06/0922_fixing_finance_baily_litan.pdf

Berwick, D.M., James, B., Coye, M.J. Connections between quality measurement and improvement. *Med Care.* 2003;41:I30–8.

Campanella, P., Vukovic, V., Parente, P. et al. "The Impact of Public Reporting on Clinical Outcomes: A Systematic Review and Meta-Analysis". *BMC Health Serv Res* 2016;16:296.

Commonwealth Fund. "How Medical Debt Makes People Sicker - and What We Can Do About It," The Dose, Joel Bervell. Published October 27, 2023. Last Accessed February 7, 2024. Available at: https://www.commonwealthfund.org/publications/podcast/2023/oct/how-medical-debt-makes-people-sicker-what-we-can-do-about-it

Cordina, J., Greenberg, S. "Consumer Decision Making in Healthcare: The Role of Information Transparency". McKinsey & Company, July 2020. Last Accessed January 24, 2024. Available at: https://www.mckinsey.com/industries/healthcare/our-insights/consumer-decision-making-in-healthcare-the-role-of-information-transparency

Energy and Commerce Committee of the House of Representatives. "Nearly 90 Percent of Americans Support Health Care Transparency". Published July 11, 2023. Last Accessed January 24, 2024. Available at: https://energycommerce.house.gov/posts/nearly-90-percent-of-americans-support-health-care-price-transparency

Kaiser Family Foundation. "Ongoing Challenges with Hospital Price Transparency". Published February 10, 2023. Last Accessed February 7, 2024. Available at: https://www.kff.org/health-costs/issue-brief/ongoing-challenges-with-hospital-price-transparency/#:~:text=This%20analysis%20examines%20transparency%20data,them%20for%20their%20intended%20purpose

Kroszner, R. S. "Prospects for Recovery and Repair of Mortgage Markets." Presented at the *Annual Conference of State Bank Supervisors*, Amelia Island, Plantation, FL, May 22, 2008. Last Accessed February 27, 2024. Available at: http://www.federalreserve.gov/newsevents/speech/kroszner20080522a.htm

Morris, L. "How Patients Use Online Reviews", Master Patient Experience Survey 2020, Software Advice. Published April 3, 2020. Last Accessed January 24, 2024. Available at: https://www.softwareadvice.com/resources/how-patients-use-online-reviews/#back

Sinaiko, A., Bambury, E., and Chien, A. "Consumer Choice in U.S. Health Care: Using Insights from the Past to Inform the Way Forward". Commonwealth Fund, November 2021.

Chapter 9

Healthcare Transformer 3: Strategy

New and emerging entities in healthcare are continuing to capture traditional markets and develop novel platforms and services. These forces are both innovative and disruptive to existing healthcare organizations. While every organization will say that they have a strategy, not every strategic approach is consistent or adaptive in the face of these changes. Additionally, strategies without measurable goals (long-term and short-term) are meaningless. Without specific targets, how does an organization know if they have achieved their strategies? In the increasingly fast-paced and rapidly evolving healthcare system it is essential to not only have key strategies and goals but also the foresight to understand when to revise and shift that strategic plan (Figure 9.1).

In this chapter, HealthCare Transformer 3 details the importance of establishing and maintaining a meaningful and agile strategic approach within the organization and through all its efforts.

Problem

A fundamental Board role is the engagement in developing key strategies to achieve the organizational mission. Strategy requires careful consideration of market dynamics, internal organizational assessment of capabilities, and anticipation for the future. Yet, recent decades have brought a flood of more, in terms of more information, service lines, competition, quality measures, staff distribution,

DOI: 10.4324/9781003493914-9

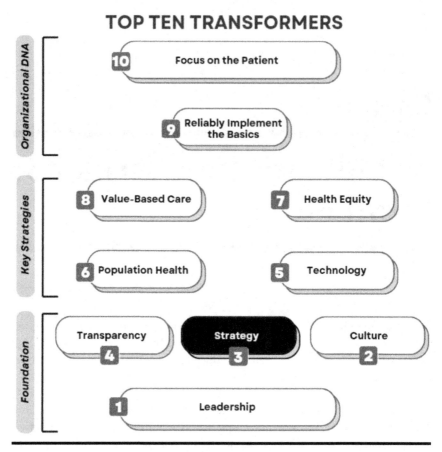

Figure 9.1   Top ten healthcare transformers.

and other healthcare industry confounders. Board members are thus left with the challenge of consuming and digesting more data and information without necessarily adding more meeting time. As a result, intentional efforts to discuss, process, and strategically plan are at risk. Among several trends that challenge successful strategic planning, consider the following:

- **Time:** One recent study found that 71% of all hospital Boards spend less than half of Board meeting time in active deliberation and debate (AHA 2019). There is simply more information to review and less time to talk about each area and issue.
- **Innovation:** More than 75% of hospital Boards have low levels of board member turnover. A further 61% have no board member continuing

education requirements, and a third do not have term limits. Meanwhile, Boards continue to observe slow progress in their racial, ethnic, and gender diversity. More than 9 out of 10 (91%) Boards are interested in identifying and engaging more board candidates who represent more diverse characteristics. Each of these factors limits the introduction of new ideas, energy, and points of view (AHA 2023).

■ **Disruption:** The healthcare sector has seen massive investment by private equity as well as consolidation of traditional healthcare systems. These are in new and emerging areas, and not necessarily among traditional geographic lines. In the 2010s over 1500 hospitals were targeted for acquisition, and more than 55% were not located within the same commuting zone (Navathe & Connolly 2023). This has led to a market that has and continues to evolve in a way that requires constant evaluation and re-evaluation of organizational strategic focus.

These disruptive forces occur when a change or sequence of changes challenges current systems to the point that incumbents operating within them cannot adapt to that change. Board members must be prepared for innovation and disruption to the extent to which they become the anticipated norm. Successful organizations are adept at sifting through large amounts of information and translating this into meaningful goals, actions, and improvements. At the core of this transformation is intentional and dedicated strategic planning.

Transformer

In the past, healthcare organizations could count on holding a strategic planning session to set a long-term strategic target, and then step back for several years as it played out. In the meantime, Boards could focus principally on financial stewardship in between the development of such strategic plans. The modern healthcare climate no longer allows such a 'set it and forget it' approach. Boards must look beyond traditional strategic planning, and consider vision and organizational strategy as ongoing and dynamic elements of their work. This requires the ability to adapt in response to changing climates and unexpected market factors. Boards should adopt the following principles in all of their strategic planning:

■ **Divide and Conquer:** There is no one-size-fits-all approach to strategy. Board members should be prepared to consider segmenting how their organization delivers care and be willing to vary strategies within these different segments.

- **Continually Challenge Assumptions:** Organizations cannot expect to wait to see how competitors perform and passively respond to changes in the market. Board members should anticipate and proactively consider new technologies, processes, and delivery modalities. Likewise, they should continually challenge and question their current processes and environments.
- **Think Outside the Box:** Traditional models of healthcare delivery and siloed care have limitations. As new entities emerge, board members should seek to consider if there are new partnerships or connections that their organization should be investing in.
- **Set Bold Goals:** Effective strategic plans have measurable strategic goals. However, it is additionally important to have bold enough strategic goals. Setting an aspirational goal sends a message in terms of its importance and also drives strategy. Do you want to improve your patient experience by being in the top quartile in your state in five years or do you want to be in the top decile in the nation? The discussion of these goals and how to get there is the heart of strategy development and deployment.
- **Deeply Connect to Annual Operating Plans:** The visionary 5- or 10-year strategic plans provide a roadmap. However, they must be connected to annual operating plans. The annual operating plans have key actions and short-term goals that must be clearly aligned with the strategies.

An essential strategy for any leader is to understand priorities and what really matters for their organization and patients. A particular challenge for board members is that the amount of information presented to them can be overwhelming, and the healthcare industry is simultaneously complex and convoluted. Thus, a necessary strategy and critical governance competency is to be able to detect and differentiate signal from noise. This means being able to identify what is meaningful information (signal) from random or unwanted variation (noise) that interferes or hinders the signal. The Governance Institute identified four actions to focus board members on signals (Critchfield & Joshi 2023):

1. **Goal Setting:** When setting goals, consider historical performance and also where your organization stands compared to peers. While improvement may be happening - is it occurring fast enough? An example is an organization's intent to improve provider response time to patient portal messages. If the organization's baseline for the previous year was that 40% of all messages were answered within 24 hours, a reasonable appearing goal may be to aim to improve this to 60%. However, if the national average is actually 75%, this changes the context of what to strive for.
2. **Measures:** When reviewing data, be certain to pay attention to aggregate measures of performance, not just individual discrete measures. An individual measure may be the rate of falls with injury or the number of

surgical site infections, while the aggregate measure is the goal of reducing total patient harm. At times, the success of one small metric can become loud noise that can drown out the reality that more global outcomes that truly matter are not being met.

3. **Long-Term Planning:** Goals effectively serve as artificial floors or ceilings that teams will either aspire toward or settle with. When planning for the future, board members should aim for big goals that lead to redesign, restructuring, or reimagining, as opposed to incremental improvement. In this way, the strategic planning process itself can generate clear signals to the organization about new and high ceilings, as opposed to producing more noise.

4. **Mission and Key Strategies:** Connect everything in the organizational mission to key strategies. Board agendas and discussions should not only be meaningful but also align with these strategies. When organizational action does not link to mission, vision, or value, it inherently creates more noise.

Effectively detecting signals from noise allows the organization to identify what matters, focus improvement, and eliminate waste and distraction. Staying out of the 'weeds', in other words being too mired in details and specific actions, is a key driver for strategic success.

Best Practices

Strategy is a foundation for connecting organizational mission with prioritized resources through initiatives to achieve impact on those served. Board members should collaborate with senior leaders to aggressively pursue bold initiatives to improve health. The process to do so should consider differing opinions and community benefits among financial implications.

Setting Bold Initiatives

Go Big or Go Home: One effort that Boards can engage in is to leverage their strategic and fiduciary responsibility and the organization's financial resources and truly think big. If the organization wanted to use a major part of its financial resources, such as one-third of its financial reserves, what big strategies could the organization consider? This is not to say they should implement those strategies. But as a Board, considering this approach provides a real opportunity to think big and identify strategies that would normally not surface. Allowing one to think about using a major part of their financial resources opens up more strategic possibilities.

Meritus Health conducted a strategic planning exercise among the organization's senior leadership to assess potential initiatives each individual felt could

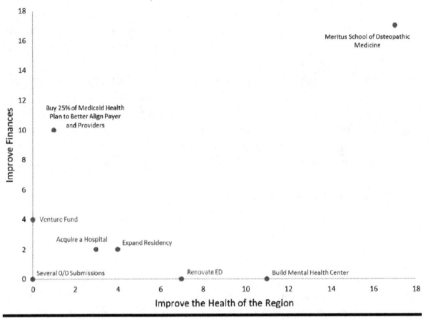

Figure 9.2 Meritus health strategic planning exercise financial and community benefit matrix. The horizontal axis recognizes the value of improving the health of the region while the vertical access depicts financial impact. In the grid a higher score demonstrates greater potential for value or financial improvement. (Meritus Health, Hagerstown, MD, as cited in Feldmiller 2022).

provide significant benefit to the community. Each leader was given a hypothetical $100 million and was asked to list three specific ideas for community investment. The ideas were all collected, and the rationale behind each was shared. Following, each senior leader was given a total of 12 points to award to prioritized items in the categories of "improving finances" and "improving the health of the region". Each idea was arranged into the grid displayed in Figure 9.2, and this matrix was reviewed by the strategic planning committee. This allowed the ability to visualize the intersection between financial implications and community impact and led to the investment of $160 million in the development of the Meritus School of Osteopathic Medicine, which was initiated following this strategic planning exercise (Feldmiller & Joshi 2022).

Setting Long-Term Strategic Goals

There are many examples of bold goals that organizations are setting in their strategic plans. Examples include:

- Having zero suicides in your community
- Losing one million pounds in your community
- Being a nationally ranked employer of choice
- Eliminating infant and maternal mortality
- Achieving zero patient harm
- Being the lowest cost in your state (as measured by cost per admission)
- Ensuring all patients can see a primary provider on the same day

Board Questions

As a health system board member, consider these questions:

1. Do we know the biggest competitive threats facing our organization and the biggest internal weaknesses?
2. Do we have three to five long-term strategies that we are revisiting at least every three years to ensure they are relevant?
3. What are the long-term goals for each of our strategies?
4. Are there any emerging or future competitors whose impact we should be considering?
5. Are we bold enough in our strategies and in our goals?
6. If you wanted to spend one-third of your financial reserves on a major strategy, what would you do?

References

American Hospital Association (AHA). "National Health Care Governance Survey Report". AHA Trustee Services. 2019. Last Accessed March 1, 2014. Available at: https://trustees.aha.org/system/files/media/file/2019/06/aha-2019-governance-survey-report_v8-final.pdf

American Hospital Association (AHA). "Hospital Boards are Adapting to Changing Times". Published February 6, 2023. Last Accessed March 1, 2024. Available at: https://www.aha.org/news/blog/2023-02-06-hospital-boards-are-adapting-changing-times

Critchfield, C.N., Joshi, M.S. "Detecting Signal from Noise: A Critical Governance Competency". Governance Institute, Board Room Press, December 2023. 1–2.

Feldmiller, E., Joshi, M.S. "Go Big or Go Home: A Board Framework for Strategic Planning of Big Ideas". Governance Institute, Board Room Press, December 2022. 1–2.

Navathe, A.S., Connolly, J.E. "Hospital Consolidation: The Rise of Geographically Distant Mergers". *JAMA*. 2023;329(18):1547–1548.

Chapter 10

Healthcare Transformer 2: Culture

Culture is the most often spoken barrier to improving healthcare and, yet, perhaps the least well-understood. Culture is the way things are done in an organization and is reflective of behaviors, norms, and beliefs. Healthcare transformation will not occur unless the culture of the industry and healthcare organizations also transform (see Figure 10.1). An often-quoted phrase is that "culture eats strategy for lunch," symbolizing that all change plans are meaningless if they counter the prevailing cultural norm. Rather that strategy develops from and upon a foundation of strong culture. Dramatic change starts, includes, and ends with culture.

Problem

The lack of a positive (open, "no-blame") culture is extremely detrimental to the quality of care and patient safety, as seen in the following study:

- In a 2022 survey of hospital healthcare members, 35% of patient safety events that were caught and corrected before reaching the patient, and 17% that did reach the patient and could have caused harm, were never reported. In the same report, almost 1 out of every 4 times an error occurred (24%), there was no communication or discussion on ways to prevent them from happening again (Hare et al. 2022).

DOI: 10.4324/9781003493914-10

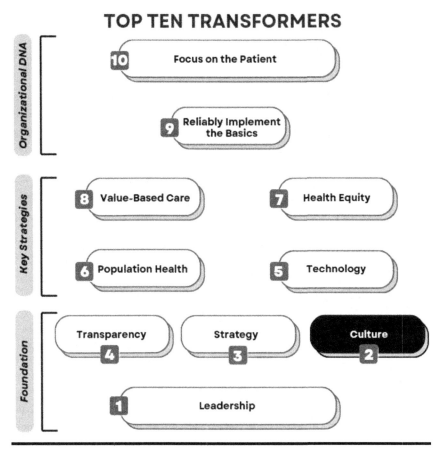

Figure 10.1 Top ten healthcare transformers.

Recently, Vaughn et al. (2019) carried out an extensive review showing that across a wide range of healthcare settings, the single characteristic most associated with struggling healthcare organizations is poor organizational culture. Major contributors to this included limited ownership by leaders and team members, uncollaborative environments and communication, hierarchical structure, and disconnected leadership (Vaught et al. 2019). Previous studies have identified the importance of culture and organizational climate (MacDavitt et al. 2007):

■ Leadership, group behavior (coordination and communication), and conflict management were directly associated with employee satisfaction, lower nurse turnover, and higher perceived quality of patient care.

- Leadership (safety climate characterized by safety procedure, flow of safety information, and organizational priority of safety) was associated with higher rates of treatment error reports.
- Nurse-physician relationships were associated with lower mortality rates.

In healthcare, as in other industries, culture can often be confused with attitude and allowances. In other words, organizations will encourage 'casual Fridays', themed costumes and events, free coffee in the cafeteria, and other visible elements in the name of culture. True culture does permeate the working environment and these are important to establish as an investment in joy at work. However, the roots of culture in an organization are far more than the tone of those who work in a place or the guidelines that they follow. As Edgar Shein of MIT, one of the world's leading experts on organizational culture puts it:

> Culture is a way of working together toward common goals that have been followed so frequently and so successfully that people don't even think about trying to do things another way. If a culture has formed, people will autonomously do what they need to do to be successful.

> (Christenson 2012)

Transformer

The transformer opportunity includes defining your organization's desired culture. Your organization must clearly state the culture it seeks to foster, which could be patient-centered, ensuring a high-reliability culture towards patient safety or striving for a culture of agility and innovation. Elements of a desired culture include:

- Reflecting the desired culture in your strategic plan
- Ensuring your annual operating plan has metrics related to evidence of the desired culture in place
- An agenda item at periodic board and management meetings to reflect on progress toward the culture
- Accountability by recognizing culture as a major factor in the performance evaluation of managers and staff
- Having policies and systems to enforce the desired behaviors. For example, you may have a policy on Just Culture if you desire a safety-focused culture
- Teamwork is generally the hallmark of any specified culture in healthcare, and it is thus essential to have robust training related to teamwork that focuses on communication, handoffs, conflict management, and decision-making

Best Practices

The following are practices that have been shown to create a positive organizational culture or climate for quality and patient safety:

Delineation of Patient Safety Priorities

Organizations should clearly specify their priorities in patient safety to motivate staff and target improvement efforts. For example, The Joint Commission has identified the following patient safety priorities as a part of their National Patient Safety Goals for Hospitals (Joint Commission 2023):

- Improve the accuracy of patient identification
- Improve the effectiveness of communication among caregivers
- Improve the safety of using medications
- Reduce patient harm associated with clinical alarm systems
- Reduce the risk of healthcare-associated infections
- The hospital identifies safety risks inherent in its patient population
- Improve healthcare equity

The Agency for Healthcare Research and Quality (AHRQ) has developed surveys that allow organizations to assess such critical variables affecting culture as communication, supervision, and willingness to report medical errors. Initially designed in 2004, these were updated in 2019 to allow organizations to be compared with others to examine the effectiveness of cultural change efforts. Topics covered in the survey are depicted in Figure 10.2, and the survey itself can be found at https://www.ahrq.gov/sops/surveys/hospital/index.html (AHRQ 2023a).

Fair and Just Culture

The Dana Farber Cancer Institute (DFCI) has included individual accountability in its patient safety culture. DFCI has a policy that states:

> A fair and just culture means giving constructive feedback and critical analysis in skilful ways, doing assessments that are based on facts, and having respect for the complexity of the situation. It also means providing fair-minded treatment, having productive conversations, and creating effective structures that help people reveal their errors and help the organization learn from them...DFCI commits to holding individuals accountable for their own performance in accordance with their job responsibilities and the DFCI core values. However, individuals should not carry the burden for system flows over which they had no control.
>
> (Conner et al. 2007)

Topics Covered by SOPS Hospital Survey 2.0
Composite Measures: A composite measure is a grouping of two or more survey items that assess the same area of culture. The 10 composite measures and 32 survey items assessed in the SOPS Hospital Survey 2.0 are:
Teamwork (3 items)
Staffing and Work Pace (4 items)
Organizational Learning - Continuous Improvement (3 items)
Response to Error (4 items)
Supervisor, Manager, or Clinical Leader Support for Patient Safety (3 items)
Communication About Error (3 items)
Communication Openness (4 items)
Reporting Patient Safety Events (2 items)
Hospital Management Support for Patient Safety (3 items)
Handoffs and Information Exchange (3 items)
Additional Measures: In addition to the composite measures, single item measures included assess:
Number of events reported (1 item)
Patient safety rating (1 item)
Background questions (4 items)

Figure 10.2   **Topics covered in the survey on patient safety culture. (Agency for Healthcare Research and Quality Rockville, MD, 2023).**

"Near Miss" Meetings

This meeting or an agenda item at a quality improvement or staff meeting is designed to be a no-blame, open discussion of errors that were caught or nearly made. A quality professional or a designated person on the unit or service usually facilitates this meeting. Individuals are encouraged and even rewarded for identifying the near miss, and a discussion ensues on ways to prevent the potential error in the future.

TeamSTEPPS

In 2006, the Department of Defense Patient Safety Program released Team Strategies and Tools to Enhance Performance and Patient Safety (TeamSTEPPS). The program incorporates more than 30 years of research on team development and performance across all industries and has been utilized extensively in health care (AHRQ 2023b). Updated as TeamSTEPPS 3.0 in 2023, the program includes an evidence-based collection of tools, strategies, and training curriculum focused on establishing high-performing teams through:

- Producing highly effective medical teams that optimize the use of information, people, and resources to achieve the best clinical outcomes for patients;
- Increasing team awareness and clarifying team roles and responsibilities;
- Resolving conflicts and improving information sharing; and
- Eliminating barriers to quality and safety.

The TeamSTEPPS curriculum includes four key principles: communication, team leadership, situation monitoring, and mutual support. As depicted in Figure 10.3, the curriculum emphasizes the dynamic, two-way relationship between outcomes (performance, knowledge, attitudes) and skills encircled by the patient care team. The patient care team includes not only those directly responsible for providing medical care but also all of those on and off the medical staff (i.e., family members and caregivers) who are involved in the patient's care as Figure 10.4 depicts.

Figure 10.3   TeamSTEPPS framework and competencies. (Agency for Healthcare Research & Quality, Rockville, MD, 2023).

TeamSTEPPS Key Principles
Communication
SBAR (Situation, Background, Assessment, Recommendation or Request)
Closed-Loop Communication
Call-Out
Check-Back
Teach-Back
Handoff
I-PASS
Team Leadership
Huddle
Brief Checklist
Debrief Checklist
Situation Monitoring
STEP
I'M SAFE Checklist
Cross-Monitoring
STAR (Stop, Think, Act, Review)
Mutual Support
Task Assistance
Formative Feedback
Advocacy and Assertion
Two-Challenge Rule
CUS (Concerned, Uncomfortable, Safety)
DESC (Describe, Express, Suggest, Consequences)

Figure 10.4 TeamSTEPPS key principles. (Agency for Healthcare Research & Quality, Rockville, MD, 2023).

Board Questions

As a health system board member, consider these questions:

1. Have we defined our desired culture of high performance?
2. Have measures and goals of a desired culture been delineated for the organization?
3. Are we evaluating responses to culture surveys by physicians, nurses, and administrators to assess differences?
4. What are the top cultural changes we are trying to change and how?
5. How are we strategically and tactically trying to improve teamwork?

References

Agency for Healthcare Research and Quality. Hospital Survey on Patient Safety Culture. Content last reviewed March 2023a. Rockville, MD. Last Accessed February 27, 2024. Available at: https://www.ahrq.gov/sops/surveys/hospital/index.html

Agency for Healthcare Research and Quality. TeamSTEPPS 3.0: Team Strategies & Tools to Enhance Performance and Patient Safety. AHRQ Pub. No. 23 0043. Published May 2023b. Last Accessed February 27, 2024. Available at: https://www.ahrq.gov/sites/default/files/wysiwyg/teamstepps-program/teamstepps-pocket-guide.pdf

Christenson, C. *How Will You Measure Your Life.* HarperCollins Publishers: New York, NY. 2012, 160.

Conner, M., D. Duncombe, E. Barclay, S. Bartel, E. Gross, C. Miller, P. Reid Ponte. "Creating a Fair and Just Culture: One Institution's Path toward Organizational Change." *Jt Comm J Qual Patient Saf* 2007;33:617–624.

Joint Commission. "National Patient Safety Goals: Effective January 2024 for the Hospital Program. Published October 4, 2023. Last Accessed January 26, 2024. Available at: https://www.jointcommission.org/-/media/tjc/documents/standards/national-patient-safety-goals/2024/npsg_chapter_hap_jan2024.pdf

Hare, R., Tapia, A., Tyler, E.R., Fan, L., Ji, S., Yount, N.D., et al. "Surveys on Patient Safety CultureTM (SOPS®) Hospital Survey 2.0: 2022 User Database Report." (Prepared by Westat, Rockville, MD, under Contract No. HHSP233201500026I/HHSP23337004T). Rockville, MD: Agency for Healthcare Research and Quality; October 2022. AHRQ Publication No. 22(23)-0066.

MacDavitt, K., S. Chou, P. Stone. "Organizational Climate and Health Care Outcomes." *Jt Comm J Qual Patient Saf* 2007;33(11):45–56.

Vaughn, V.M., Saint, S., Krein, S.L., Forman, J.H., Meddings, J., Ameling, et al. "Characteristics of Healthcare Organisations Struggling to Improve Quality: Results from a Systematic Review of Qualitative Studies." *BMJ Qual Saf.* 2019;28(1):74–84.

Chapter 11

Healthcare Transformer 1: Leadership

Leadership is the key to organizational performance and thus appropriately identified as Transformer 1 in Figure 11.1. In other words, this can be viewed as the foundation for all other work for the Board as well as for the organization and teams. Leaders can drive *transformational change*—that is, changes in values and patterns of behavior so that healthcare organizations can address long-standing performance and quality issues. Effective leadership is a critical lever for dramatically improving the performance of an organization and cumulatively, the industry. The Baldrige National Quality Award, in its healthcare criteria for performance excellence, identifies leadership as its first criterion and states that leaders should set an organizational vision, create a customer focus, demonstrate clear and visible values and ethics, and set high expectations for the workforce (NIST 2023).

Problem

The need for leadership to transform healthcare systems can be seen in the following:

- Despite decades of emphasis on quality and safety, there are still an estimated 1.2 million individuals harmed each year by medical errors in hospitals in the United States (Toussaint & Segel 2022).

DOI: 10.4324/9781003493914-11

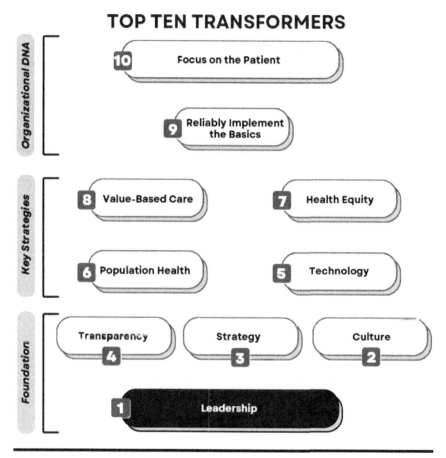

Figure 11.1 Top ten healthcare transformers

- Staffing, recruitment, and teamwork require strong leadership to create a supportive and positive work environment. Nationally, hospitals turnover an average of 22.7% of their workforce annually (NSI 2023). Though impacted by the pandemic, 2021 alone saw the exit of over 330,000 providers from the workforce (Gamble 2022).
- A 2019 survey by the Joint Commission found nearly 8 of 10 healthcare professionals cited a lack of leadership (77%) and absence of organizational investment (79%) contributing to barriers to patient safety (Benedicto 2019).
- Most medical errors are caused not by individual incompetence but by poor systems and processes that are under the control of leaders throughout the organization. In his classic book, *Out of the Crisis*, Deming says, "Workers work in the system. Leaders work on the system." (Deming 1986).

Leadership is core for well-coordinated and integrated care, from the view of both patients and healthcare professionals. Further, a multitude of studies has demonstrated that correlations exist between leadership and quality of care, including 30-day mortality rate, injuries, patient safety, patient satisfaction, level of perceived pain, use of physical restraints, and many more (Sfantou et al. 2017).

Yet, in the healthcare industry, the path to leadership itself is often unplanned and at times unexpected. Many healthcare leaders, particularly physicians and nurses, rise or are elevated to a leadership position as a result of garnering trust from colleagues through experience or clinical expertise. Frequently, this is without formal training in leadership itself. These leaders bring a wealth of expertise in how care is delivered and typically lead through reputation and relationships. Conversely, other traditional leaders and managers in healthcare, those with an education in business or management, often have no experience in direct patient care. Thus, when compared to other industries, healthcare is remarkably complex - with leadership and services that span a broad spectrum and across many areas of expertise. This underscores the vital importance of not only individual leadership but the necessity for interconnected leadership among various team members who complement each other.

Transformer

One excellent model of transformational leadership is provided by the Institute for Healthcare Improvement and depicts leadership as a complex set of five interrelated activities, encompassing 24 specific elements. As shown in Figure 11.2, these include:

1. **Set Direction:** The leader's job is to set the "future self-image" of the organization. This task can be described as creating a magnetic field whereby all members are both pulled (attracted) toward a positive future or pushed out (repelled) of the status quo.
2. **Establish the Foundation:** The foundation starts with leaders preparing themselves. It then builds with the education of their teams with knowledge and skills to improve healthcare systems and manage the change process. In addition, leaders must establish the values and practices necessary to ensure quality and patient safety.
3. **Build Will:** Leaders must overcome the comfort of the status quo and build commitment to a new culture of quality improvement and patient safety. Ways to do this include emphasizing quality at all management meetings, showing the business case (financial benefits) of improvement initiatives, having incentives for quality improvements, and holding all leaders accountable for making the transformation.

Figure 11.2   IHI framework for leadership for improvement. (From Reinertsen J.L., M. Bisognano, M.D. Pugh. *Seven Leadership Leverage Points for Organization-Level Improvement in Health Care (Second Edition)*. IHI Innovation Series White Paper. Cambridge, MA: Institute for Healthcare Improvement; 2008).

4. **Generate Ideas:** Innovation is necessary to address quality and safety issues. Effective leaders look for ideas and best practices from other organizations and the literature. They also have mechanisms to solicit ideas from their staff. These ideas and practices (whether from external or internal sources) are rapidly tested and adapted/implemented as appropriate.

5. **Execute Change:** Leaders should use and promulgate a clear model for improvement design and redesign such as the Plan-Do-Study-Act cycle, ensure that lessons learned from improvement projects get disseminated in the organization, have a clear performance metric to assess the effectiveness of change efforts, and reinforce that continuous quality improvement is everyone's job in the organization (Reinersten et al. 2008).

Organizations must be prepared to do more than just talk about and support the concept of leadership, but also to dedicate resources and infrastructure to leadership development. One 2021 study demonstrated an association between hospitals and health systems that invested in leadership development and organizational creditworthiness in the form of bond rating. Leadership practices most strongly and significantly associated with trust and a higher bond rating were found to be (Garland et al. 2021):

- Attracting and selecting leaders
- Preparing new leaders for success
- Providing performance feedback
- Incorporating administrative fellowships
- Monitoring and achieving results
- Developing clinical leadership strength

Best Practices

Leadership is what occurs when the rubber meets the road as culture and strategy take action. Likewise, great leadership reinforces culture and strategy and requires intentionality and dedication. Poor leadership arises when frameworks and expectations are not established or not followed through.

Leadership Framework

Leveraging best practices, Meritus Health has implemented a leadership framework to drive quality that engages all leaders and staff (Adams & Joshi 2021). The framework features a 10-year strategic plan with four bold goals that are supported by measurable annual goals that are linked to each of the four aims and tracked as part of a 3-year strategic plan that can be adjusted as needed. The model features True North metrics and robust process improvement elements.

Meritus Health combines the bold aspirational goals with "small ball" improvement initiatives that build to the long-term major goals. There are seven elements of the improvement initiatives, all driven by leadership:

1. **Alignment:** Regardless of the content of the plan, all staff and providers must be aligned toward the same goals and strategies. Rowing in the same direction is the analogy most often thought of for alignment.
2. **Improvement:** The success of any improvement effort is the discipline and rigor in carrying out the work. Meritus uses Kata as an improvement methodology and its associated elements of rounding and training to drive improvement projects; however, any improvement method is appropriate if implemented effectively.
3. **Tools, Knowledge, and Training:** A foundation for any initiative's success is having the tools to carry out the work and having the knowledge through training to support continuous learning. Meritus invested in a small team

of three full-time employees to be expertly trained in process improvement and coaching for outcomes. More than 50 managers and supervisors leading improvement projects dedicate approximately 30–60 minutes each day to meet with their coach and implement change ideas. Additional quality improvement courses were created, internally, to train leaders in data fluency, driver diagrams, and change interventions. These investments ensure leaders have resources and access to tools for success.

4. **Visual Management:** Physical visual management allows a rapid and continuous opportunity to share information — in a communal location — that can be used to track ongoing performance.

5. **Dashboards and Transparency:** Having a comprehensive and focused set of performance measures that are reported and discussed frequently is a hallmark of improvement.

6. **True North Metrics:** As it sounds, the True North metrics provide the guide to always help the organization navigate toward its long-term mission and the "why" behind all of the small initiatives.

7. **Leader and Patient Rounding:** The traditional leadership principle of managing by walking and connecting with team members is advanced in the organization with a specific purpose and structure to further the patient experience and Kata improvement.

As a specific leader example, the practice of sit-down, face-to-face weekly three-hour senior leader meetings were eliminated. In place of that meeting time, the senior executive team huddles 5 days a week, for 15 minutes maximum each day at 8 a.m. Each daily huddle includes a focus on specific areas, including performance metrics (Metric Monday), sharing learning sessions that are critical to operations (Teaching Tuesday), weekly individual goals or sprints (Whirlwind Wednesday), and recommendations for approval and communications (Tracker Thursday), with an open-themed session at the end of the week (Freeform Friday).

Board Questions

As a health system board member, consider these questions:

1. Do you have a framework or model of leadership you consider in driving performance?
2. Are all leaders held accountable for quality and are they rewarded when improvements have been made?
3. Do you hold leadership accountable for quality performance at the same level as financial performance?

4. Do you expect leadership to possess the same experience and expertise in quality as compared to finance?
5. Are there programs in place to develop leaders and staff in quality improvement?
6. How does our organization develop and promote leaders?
7. Are there any types of leaders or leadership roles that our organization is lacking to achieve your performance goals?

References

Adams, C., Joshi, M. "Bold Goals and Small Initiatives: A Framework for Improvement". *NEJM Catal Innov Care Deliv* 2021;2(11). DOI: 10.1056/CAT.21.0075

Benedicto, A. "Commentary: Healthcare Remains Unprepared for Today's Complex Challenges". *Modern Healthcare*. Published August 31, 2019. Last Accessed January 24, 2024. Accessible at: https://www.modernhealthcare.com/opinion/healthcare-unprepared-todays-complex-challenges

Deming, W. E. *Out of the Crisis*. Cambridge, MA: MIT Press, 1986.

Gamble, M. "Healthcare Workforce Lost 333,942 Providers in 2021". *Becker's Hospital Review*. Published October 24, 2022. Last Accessed January 24, 2024. Available at: https://www.beckershospitalreview.com/workforce/healthcare-workforce-lost-333-942-providers-in-2021.html

Garland, N., Garman, A. N., O'Neil, S., Jeffrey, C. W. "The Impact of Hospital and Health System Leadership Development Practices on Bond Ratings". *Journal of Healthcare Management*, 2021;66(1), 63–74.

National Institute of Standards and Technology (NIST). Baldrige Performance Excellence Framework (Health Care): 2023–2024. 2023.

NSI Nursing Solutions, "2023 NSI National Health Care Retention & RN Staffing Report". Published March 2023. Last Accessed January 24, 2024. Available at: https://www.nsinursingsolutions.com/Documents/Library/NSI_National_Health_Care_Retention_Report.pdf

Reinertsen J.L., Bisognano, M., Pugh, M.D. Seven Leadership Leverage Points for Organization-Level Improvement in Health Care (Second Edition). *IHI Innovation Series White Paper*. Cambridge, MA: Institute for Healthcare Improvement. 2008.

Sfantou, D.F., Laliotis, A., Patelarou, A.E., Sifaki-Pistolla, D., Matalliotakis, M., Patelarou, E. "Importance of Leadership Style Towards Quality of Care Measures in Healthcare Settings: A Systematic Review". *Healthcare (Basel)*. 2017;5(4):73.

Toussaint, J., Segel, K. "4 Actions to Reduce Medical Errors in U.S. Hospitals". *Harvard Business Review*. Published April 20, 2022. Last Accessed January 24, 2024. Available at: https://hbr.org/2022/04/4-actions-to-reduce-medical-errors-in-u-s-hospitals#:~:text=In%20the%20021%20years%20since,errors%20made%20in%20U.S.%20hospitals

Chapter 12

The Big Questions for Your Organization and Healthcare Transformation

This concluding chapter provides a compilation of the questions a Board member should ask relative to their organization and healthcare transformation. This list of over 50 questions serves as a toolkit for active and engaged dialogue at the governance level. As Board members, knowing how healthcare can transform, how it impacts your organization and what you can ask and discuss to be strong stewards of the organization makes you a valuable and essential Board member. Thank you for taking on this important fiduciary role and your desire to continuously learn and contribute to the mission of your organization in a transforming industry.

The Big Questions Board Members Should Ask

Transformer 10: Focus on the Patient (Chapter 2)

1. Does our organization deliver care to every patient in the way I would want for myself, a family member, or a friend?
2. What are our biggest gaps and improvement opportunities in patient-centeredness?

DOI: 10.4324/9781003493914-12

3. How are patients and families involved in the design of our improvement efforts?
4. How are patients and families engaged in their care?
5. Are there evidenced-based patient-centered interventions that we should try implementing; for example, sharing patient stories of medical errors and near misses at leadership and board meetings, providing apologies, disclosing errors, including patients on improvement teams, and cultivating patient and family advisory councils?

Transformer 9: Reliably Implement the Basics (Chapter 3)

1. How are we doing in implementing and disseminating tried-and-true best practices?
2. How do our results compare to, not only to state and national averages but to benchmarks – such as the top decile or quartile?
3. Have we learned from the best-performing organizations that have achieved benchmark performance?
4. What are the major lessons (successes and failures) from our recent quality improvement initiatives?
5. What are our biggest barriers to the adoption of best practices, and what specific strategies are we using to overcome those barriers?
6. Is quality improvement a necessary competency for professional advancement and for leadership?

Transformer 8: Value-Based Care (Chapter 4)

1. How does our organization measure value in our care delivery?
2. What is our organization doing to lower costs?
3. What is the extent of fee-for-service care that your organization participates in?
4. What are the (financial and non-financial) incentives for our clinicians to provide high-quality care?
5. Are there any new value-based care arrangements that we should consider with partners or health plans?
6. What gaps or opportunities exist in our current performance that are limiting higher-value healthcare delivery?

Transformer 7: Health Equity (Chapter 5)

1. Have we stratified our quality data by important demographic variables (race, ethnicity, language spoken, and others important to our population)?

2. What specific disparities in care do we have in our population?
3. Do we have teams with action plans working to reduce specific disparities in care?
4. How do the leadership and team members in our organization align with the demographics of the population we serve?
5. In what ways does our strategic plan address enhancing diversity, equity, and inclusion?
6. Does every member of our team, including leadership and frontline workers, go through unconscious bias training?

Transformer 6: Population Health (Chapter 6)

1. How does our organization develop and implement population health initiatives?
2. For which patient populations can we be providing better value?
3. What is an example of a health inequity that we sought to improve with a population health approach?
4. Which non-medical care factors that impact health status are we addressing the most and what factor is next?
5. Which social determinants of health are we impacting the most?
6. How do we prioritize different population health initiatives in our organization?

Transformer 5: Technology (Chapter 7)

1. What is our technology strategy and operating plan?
2. Are we on track with the implementation of our various technology systems?
3. Approximately what percentage of our workflow is not paperless?
4. Are there other innovative or disruptive organizations in our marketplace or community that are using technologies that we do not?
5. How do patients access their medical records and connect with their healthcare team, and are there opportunities to improve?
6. How is, or will, our organization apply artificial intelligence to deliver care?

Transformer 4: Transparency (Chapter 8)

1. How does our organization compare on publicly reported indicators?
2. Are we publishing our own data on our website? Why or why not?
3. Are we educating staff well enough on these measures and our philosophy?

4. Are we educating the community on these publicly reported quality measures?
5. Are we transparent not just on data, but on key practices and policies, such as how we collect patient payments or how we communicate medical errors?
6. Do we transparently share our prices in a way that is clear and easy to understand?

Transformer 3: Strategy (Chapter 9)

1. Do we know the biggest competitive threats facing our organization and the biggest internal weaknesses?
2. Do we have three to five long-term strategies that we are revisiting at least every three years to ensure they are relevant?
3. What are the long-term goals for each of our strategies?
4. Are there any emerging or future competitors whose impact we should be considering?
5. Are we bold enough in our strategies and in our goals?
6. If you wanted to spend one-third of your financial reserves on a major strategy, what would you do?

Transformer 2: Culture (Chapter 10)

1. Have we defined our desired culture of high performance?
2. Have measures and goals of a desired culture been delineated for the organization?
3. Are we evaluating responses to culture surveys by physicians, nurses, and administrators to assess differences?
4. What are the top cultural changes we are trying to change and how?
5. How are we strategically and tactically trying to improve teamwork?

Transformer 1: Leadership (Chapter 11)

1. Do you have a framework or model of leadership you consider in driving performance?
2. Are all leaders held accountable for quality and are they rewarded when improvements have been made?
3. Do you hold leadership accountable for quality performance at the same level as financial performance?

4. Do you expect leadership to possess the same experience and expertise in quality as compared to finance?
5. Are there programs in place to develop leaders and staff in quality improvement?
6. How does our organization develop and promote leaders?
7. Are there any types of leaders or leadership roles that our organization is lacking to achieve your performance goals?

Index

Pages in *italics* refer to figures.

Printed in the United States
by Baker & Taylor Publisher Services